LIKE FATHER, LIKE SON

Wilfrid Harrington OP

Like Father, Like Son

*'Who sees me,
sees the Father'*

DOMINICAN PUBLICATIONS

First published (2020) by
Dominican Publications
42 Parnell Square
Dublin 1

ISBN 978-1-905604-43-2

British Library Cataloguing in Publications Data.
A catalogue record for this book is available
from the British Library.

Scripture quotations are from the *New Revised Standard Version Bible,
Catholic Edition*, copyright © 1999 the Division of Christian Education
of the National Council of the Churches of Christ in the United States
of America. Used by permission. All rights reserved.

Cover design by
David Cooke

Cover images by
Bernardo Ramonfaur,
sourced from Shutterstock

Printed in Ireland by
PrintDynamics, Ballycoolin, Dublin 11

Contents

Preface

'I believe in one God, the Father, the Almighty'. We Christians solemnly profess our faith in God. One may ask: Who is this God of our faith and profession? I have become increasingly conscious of the absolute importance of our image of God – how we perceive God. Throughout an academic career of over half a century, I have written of God – the God revealed in the Old Testament and the God revealed in and by Jesus Christ. I have discerned a striking consistency in the revelation and I have perceived a wondrously attractive and deeply comforting portrait of our God.

Here, together with fresh insights, I draw on aspects of these studies. What emerges is a synthesis of some sort. Though my academic leaning has been towards the New Testament, I have, in practice, lectured on the Old Testament extensively. The result has been a comforting overall view of the Bible. In this perspective the harmony of Father and Son is manifest. Surely this ought not surprise. But I believe that it is a truth well worth stressing. This book seeks to do just that.

'Long ago God spoke to our ancestors in many and various ways by the prophets, but in these last days he has spoken to us by a Son' (Heb 1:1-2). I focus, first, on that revelation to our ancestors – on the Old Testament. Then I turn to where God has spoken his definitive word, the Word-made-flesh. Jesus of Nazareth is Immanuel – God-with-us. He is the one who has defined God. The God of his definition is the only true God. This Father of our Lord Jesus Christ is found in the Old Testament – by those who have eyes to see.

While we avoid the distraction of references and footnotes, I provide at the end two pages of 'Further Reading'. They list the names and works of scholars from whom I have garnered especially helpful insights.

Inclusion, here, of some of my own writings over the years is an indication that this modest book has, in reality, been long in its shaping. *The Prodigal Father* (Wilmington, DE: M. Glazier, 1982; *The Tears of God* (Collegeville: Liturgical Press, 1992); *God Does Care* (Dublin: Columba Press, 1994); *Hold on to Hope* (Dublin: Dominican Publications, 1998); *Seeking Spiritual Growth through the Bible* (New York: Paulist Press, 2002; *From the Presence of the Lord* (Dublin: Columba Press, 2006); *What Was Mark At? The Gospel of Mark: A Commentary* (Dublin: Columba Press, 2008); *Jesus Our Brother. The Humanity of the Lord* (New York: Paulist Press, 2010); *The Loving God* (Dublin: Columba Press, 2012); *Our Merciful God* (Dublin: Dominican Publications, 2016).

Introduction

> Long ago God spoke to our ancestors in many and various ways by the prophets, but in these last days he has spoken to us by a Son ... He is the reflection of God's glory and the exact imprint of God's very being (Heb 1:1-3).

God has spoken indeed, and we shall note something of the graciousness of his word. The promise in his words of the past has found fulfilment in the Word who is the Son. The human race stands in need of redemption. God took the initiative. He laid claim on us and has given us a claim on him. He is God for us – the living God who created us and called us to be his daughters and his sons. 'For God so loved the world that he gave his only Son' (Jn 3:16). The giving of the Son shows beyond doubt that God is in deadly earnest. In Israel the ultimate concern was God, revealed in creation and liberating intervention (the Exodus), and experienced through God's presence in Word and Spirit and Wisdom. In Christianity the ultimate value is God revealed in Jesus Christ and experienced through the gift of the Holy Spirit within the life of the church. The believing Israelite and the believing Christian strove and strive to live a life motivated by experiencing the presence of God. God has spoken and continues to speak in the Old Testament. In the New Testament God speaks through the Son. It is the same God, the one and only God. In both Testaments God's revelation is mediated through human words by humans.

But there is one vast difference. The New Testament tells of God among us in the very person of Jesus of Nazareth. In

Jesus is the fulness of revelation because in him God, in God's own self, came into our world, into our history. Our God is still Holy Mystery, shrouded now in humanness. What we term Incarnation, while wholly real, remains, essentially, mysterious. Because this matter is central, a brief venture into Christology may not go amiss.

In Jesus of Nazareth, God is really and truly present. This is the great Christian truth. But to seek to define the mysterious reality of Jesus is a precarious endeavour. Edward Schillebeecks points out: 'To attempt to define Jesus' nature is to limit it, to narrow it down, to bring it to a point that may well be too sharp, with the result that Jesus is either underestimated or overestimated.' (*God Is New Each Moment*) For centuries it has been assumed that the fifth-century Council of Chalcedon (451) had spoken the definitive christological word – all that remained was commentary. Christology became, in practice, a subtle word-game around the formula of Chalcedon. The question to be answered at Chalcedon was whether God's salvation had been given, once for all, in the man Jesus. Because the answer had to be Yes, and because salvation is of God, it had to be asserted, in the technical language of the day, that God himself was present in the man Jesus. That had been said, long before, by Paul: 'God was in Christ, reconciling the world to himself' (2 Cor 5:19).

Chalcedon gave its answer. What we, in this twenty-first century need to face is that the thought-world (Middle Platonic) and Greek terminology of Chalcedon is foreign to us, in a way that the language of Paul is not. Our English terms, nature, substance, person (these are the terms used in traditional Christology), do not mean what the corresponding Greek terms *physis, ousia, hypostasis* meant for fourth-century Greek-speakers. The situation has been aggravated by the fact that it is not Chalcedon but a certain interpretation of it that has dominated mediaeval and later Christology. People of our day and culture do not spontaneously think of approaching the mystery of Jesus by raising the question of 'nature' or 'substance'. An approach that was congenial to Christians of the fourth to the sixth centuries of our era is not so for us. We need to use a theological language we understand. Ironically, while the intention of Chalcedon was defence of the true humanity of Jesus (as the one in whom God had given salvation) the effect of the retention of its language of person and nature in the sense of the Greek – only marginally intelligible, if at all, to people of our day – has been to turn Jesus into an alien among us.

Chalcedon cannot be in contradiction with the New Testament but it certainly does not reflect the whole of New Testament Christology. On the other hand, modern Christology, if it is to be authentic, cannot contradict the Chalcedonian statement. But it must be, at very least, a reinterpretation of it. Besides, a fifth-century declaration cannot be a starting-point (as Chalcedon, in practice, had become). The starting-point of Christology has to be its historical starting-point: the New Testament. What marks Christology today is a return to New Testament categories.

Perhaps it is wisest and best to choose to live with mystery. God alone can understand how God can be wholly present in a human person. The new Testament has used 'Father' and 'Son' as the preferred way of giving expression to this ineffable truth. We would do well to be content with this.

What one seeks to do in this book is to indicate how the Son, in his life and death, gives human expression to the Father. And how the Father, by raising him from the dead, authenticates this revelation. We shall see that Jesus 'reflects the glory of God and bears the very stamp of his nature' and, yet, is 'like his brothers and sisters in every respect' (Heb 2:17).

After some general observations in this Introduction I proceed by, first, indicating some characteristics of God and, then, showing how the Son does manifest, in word and deed, the reality of the Father.

Father

The Bible is nothing other than the turbulent love-story of God and humankind. *This Tremendous Lover* is the title of a book on prayer by Irish Cistercian Eugene Boylan – an inspired title which aptly describes our God – this Tremendous Lover, too big for our pettiness. We are adept at cutting God to our measure. Happily, our paper-patterns will never translate into anything real. God, gently or painfully, sets our ways aside. Why, then, does he let us hurt ourselves and hurt others so? We need to understand that God, our Parent, has infinite respect for us. God is God of power, omnipotent – but never a God of force. His respect for his creatures, above all his human creatures, is divine. He invites us, longingly, lovingly, to respect one another. The temptation is to look through our human chaos to an uncaring God. The challenge is to find, in our troubled world, the presence of a loving God. If true love respects the one loved, what can we expect from a loving God? We need humility (another word for honesty) to learn the reality of love.

Parent and Children

God, we shall see, is the Holy One, Holy Mystery. And God is *Abba*, loving Parent. This God declares: 'I am God and there is no other; I am God and there is no one like me' (Is 46:9). Yet, God speaks to each of us: I am your *Abba*; you are my beloved child. We know that we are wholly unworthy. But our awareness of unworthiness and sinfulness does not alter the reality. God's love abides, no matter what. Humans have ever found this hard to grasp. Ironically, the staunchly religious have the greater problem. Sinners have an intuitive insight.

Jesus' parable of the Pharisee and the Tax Collector (Lk 18:9-14) is apt. The Pharisee 'trusted in himself that he was righteous'; he was comfortable with his God. The sinner was not complacent. He had been branded an outcast, warned that God had no time for him. Yet his perception, unclouded by an all-too-human image of God, did discern the true God: 'God, be merciful to me, a sinner!' He had the honesty to look at himself, at his sorry state, his radical unworthiness. And he perceived that, notwithstanding, his God loved him.

The Graciousness of God

Nothing escapes the eye of God. How regularly this observation has been cast as sanction, as threat. God does indeed keep a close eye on us – but to acknowledge whatever good we do (see Mt 6:4,6,18; 10:42). Our good works carry no price tag; there is no 'merit' in that sense. What is so much more important is 'recompense': gracious acknowledgment by a gracious God. To his eye, nothing of good that we do is unobserved or unimportant. Not surprisingly – because, wherever there is good, it is of God. There are many, very many, who feel that they do not know God. But God knows them, and rejoices in them. For one who claims to know God, it is vitally important that one know and acknowledge the true God. When I have come to know, to experience, the graciousness of God, I will not only readily discern but firmly reject anything and everything that would temper or cloud this graciousness. This asks of me that I acknowledge my God of infinite love and mercy and forgiveness.

Son

Jesus of Nazareth, the 'reflection of God's glory and the exact imprint of God's very being' is one who is, at the same time. 'like his brothers and sisters in every respect' (Heb 1:3; 2:17). Up to the launching of his brief ministry, he had lived an un-eventful life. During that public phase, he was to rouse more opposition than support. He was not immune from suffering, not even from the agony of an atrocious and humiliating death. The fact that he was 'without sin' (4:15) did not imply any lack of authentic humanness. Sin – though we all are sin-ners – is not an intrinsic ingredient of humanness. It is a fall from humanness. Jesus, then, is human in the very perfection of humanness. And here is the wonder. And here, also, is the Christian challenge: our God present in human flesh. One would argue that, if we really listen to the God of Israel across the whole spread of the Old Testament, then Paul's 'foolish' God is, indeed, the true God. And the seeming contradiction of a God in flesh and blood is God's 'wisdom'.

Defining God

Jesus had a burning desire for the renewal of the people of Israel as God's holy elect. He would not proclaim the holi-ness of God's people in cultic terms. He redefined it in terms of wholeness. Where other contemporary Jewish movements were, in their various ways, exclusive, the Jesus movement was inclusive. His challenge and his invitation were to all. What Jesus claimed was that the intervention of God expected for the End-time was, in some sort, happening in his ministry. The kingdom is here and now present in history in that the power of evil is broken, sins are forgiven, sinners are gathered into

God's friendship. The kingdom, though in its fullness still in the future, comes as present offer, in actual gift, through the proclamation of the good news.

Jesus preached the kingdom, the rule of God: he proclaimed that God is the ultimate meaning of the world. The rule of God does not signify something 'spiritual', outside of this world. Jesus was supremely concerned with our actual world. He spoke so vaguely of the future that the first Christians could expect that the end would come in their day (see 1 Thess 4:15-17; Mk 9:1; 13:20). When he preached the kingdom of God he envisaged a revolution in the existing order. He made two fundamental demands: he asked for personal conversion and he postulated a restructuring of the human world. Conversion (*metanoia*) meant changing one's mode of thinking and acting to suit God's purpose for humankind. It would be a new way of existing before God.

But conversion also meant a turning from the established order. Jesus made the point, so clearly and effectively developed by Paul, that it is not law that saves – not even the Law – it is love. Jesus' outlook and conduct were marked by freedom. His understanding of freedom is again faithfully reflected by Paul: freedom to serve. Jesus did not make life easier. His disconcerting word is that love knows no limits. He proclaimed not law but good news. The gospel is good news for one who can grasp its spirit and react positively to it. His good news embraced basic equality: all men and women, as children of the Father, are brothers and sisters. Good news so understood is a radical challenge to all social and ecclesiastical systems based on power. The kingdom of God is salvation for men and women.

In preaching the rule of God, Jesus was defining God. He proclaimed a God bent on the salvation of humankind. That is why he announced good news to the poor – the needy of every sort, the outcast. And, in the long run, it was because Jesus had proclaimed a God of overwhelming mercy that he ended up on a cross.

The Cross

It is fitting that the Cross has become the Christian symbol – fitting if it be understood. Sadly, it can be the mark of a grim, unchristian religion. Rightly, it is the mark of a love that will not count the cost: 'God so loved the world that he gave his only Son' (Jn 3:16). We must set aside our 'wisdom' and settle for the folly of God's love. If we would listen to Paul and Mark (the New Testament theologians of the Cross), indeed to all the theologians of the New Testament and to the theologians of our day who are attuned to them, then, as Paul counseled his Galatians (see Gal 4:1-7; 5:1) we would cast aside the shackles of legalism and rejoice in freedom – a Christian freedom ever circumscribed by love. And therein lies the hope of humankind. Through the freedom of love we can truly be children of the Father, can be our fully human selves. We can be images, revealers of God.

Christian Hope

Christian hope is founded on Jesus' preaching of the rule of God and on his praxis. The centrepiece of this hope is the paschal mystery of the death and resurrection of Christ. The risen Lord is, beforehand, the crucified Jesus. Christian hope resides in an historical reality including both darkness and light. It embraces both the present and the future, both this-world realities and other-world realities. We hope not only for eternal life but for justice, peace and integrity of life in this world. The ultimate purpose of God's plan for the world is not a glorified kingdom of disembodied spirits but rather a new heaven and a new earth. The Lord's Prayer makes clear that there is no heaven without earth: 'your will be done on earth as it is in heaven'. The Christian God is God of the Cross who stands in contrast to the detached Hellenistic God of omnipotence and impassibility. Biblical hope acknowledges, without remainder, the reality of suffering and makes no attempt to deny the inevitability of death. Hope acknowledges the ambiguity of human existence. It insists on life in the face of death.

CHAPTER ONE

Holy Mystery

God

A matter of supreme importance for believers is our image of God – how we perceive God. Flawed or false images abound. 'I believe in God' – we confidently make our profession of faith. But, do we pause to think what we mean by 'God'? A pervasive image of God in our day is that of a monarch who dwells on high, rules the world and judges human conduct. 'He' is the most powerful individual in the whole of reality.

At first sight this might seem acceptable. In truth, this concept of God produces a trivial image of God – that 'Man Above' – unworthy of belief. This 'God' is an aloof and distant figure. He seems to have no impact on – and little interest in – his creation. It is evident that a perception of God as distant and aloof makes it difficult, if not impossible, to have a close relationship with God. At best one might cling to a belief in the existence of a Creator. There is lack of a living faith in a Presence that might be motivation and sustenance. 'You shall love the lord your God'. My God must be lovable. Otherwise the God I worship is not the true God who loves me beyond measure for myself and as myself. And my life is immeasurably poorer.

If authentic humanness is to be achieved with and only with God, it is obviously of vital importance that one's understanding of God be true, or, at least, not overly flawed. Our talk about God is bound up with our world, bound up with talk about humankind. While we cannot *know* God, we may experience the presence of God. Because God is Creator, sustainer of all that is, there is no situation in which God is not present, no place in which he may not be found. This is why a believer can come to terms with situations that, humanly speaking, are meaningless and absurd – that remain absurd. The believer does not, in such circumstances, invoke the 'will of God'. To do so is meaningless. Human suffering and tragedy are never the will of God. What does matter is that God is never remote from our experiences. To experience the presence of God, we must let God into our lives. And this means that we must accept ourselves, we must dare to be ourselves. For to accept ourselves as we are is to open the self to accepting God as God is. Coming to terms with oneself does not mean settling for mediocrity; it is not remaining where we are.

Holy Mystery

Paradoxically, we begin to speak meaningfully of God only when we acknowledge that God is, literally, incomprehensible, that the reality of the living God is a mystery beyond all telling. God is Mystery, a Being wholly different from anything we know in our world. We simply cannot know God in God's own self. Yet, we do speak of God. Because, for us, God is personal – not some vague 'force' – we speak of God in terms of the only personality we know: human personality. But, we must constantly remind ourselves that God is not human. And we must be aware that no human word about God can be taken literally. In technical terms, we speak of God analogically.

The process works like this. One makes an affirmation: God is good. This must immediately be qualified: God is not good in the manner of creatures. The conclusion: God is Source of all good. But, what is Source of all good? In fact our human understanding of God gives us only the faintest inkling of Good that is Source of goodness. Similarly, our human understanding of love, even at its finest, can give us no real appreciation of divine love. And so on.

Metaphor

Because no human word about God can be taken literally, the language of metaphor is a privileged vehicle of God-talk. Metaphor is a figure of speech that takes the literal meaning of one known thing and extends it to shed light on something less accessible. The comparison of one term to the other is not to be taken literally but as a challenge to the imagination. An example is Jesus' words to the disciples: 'I will make you fishers of people'. We grasp the meaning; but we do not ask what, in real life, happens to fish caught in a net! Metaphor points to a reality beyond the words.

This is especially so in metaphors relating to God. So, God is Parent. God is Spouse of his people. God is Shepherd of his flock. They all speak truth of God but only when we acknowledge the purpose of metaphor. To reduce metaphor to 'plain speech' is to destroy the power of it. It is metaphor that makes biblical language so vibrant, so much more inspiring than traditional theological jargon.

God-talk

God is ever Mystery – incomprehensible. We know something of God, within the confines of human understanding. We cannot comprehend, that is, wholly grasp, the reality of God. Our theological speculation may delude us into imagining that, somehow, we do. We issue warnings on the hazard of God-language – on the need to recognise that it is always analogical. It seems that we, regularly, ignore the warning. There has been much talk about God marked by an unwarranted confidence that we know what we are talking about. We end up with a theologically neat God who does not recognise himself in our portrait of him.

If we cannot hope to comprehend God we can, however, have experience of God, through faith and in prayer. And we can speak of God and to God. God, strictly speaking, is Mystery. Yet, this gracious God has made himself known – 'for us and for our salvation' – in the words of the Creed and, ultimately, in the Word-made-flesh, Jesus of Nazareth.

Word of God

The Bible is word of God: this is acknowledged by all who take the Bible seriously. Yet, in practice, the designation – word of God – is misleading and has been, and is, the source of basic misunderstanding and has spawned a host of problems For, if the Bible is 'word of God' – what does that mean? Only humans communicate in words. This being so, when one designates a divine communication 'word of God' one is asserting that God truly does communicate with humankind. But not only so: one asserts that the form of communication is that most common form of converse among humans, the form of language. Revelation by word of God means divine revelation which has been given human expression by humans.

God has revealed himself; he has taken the initiative freely, lovingly. His revelation is invitation; he has revealed himself not for his own sake but always 'for us and for our salvation'. It is important to keep this in mind. We must realise that what we have come to learn of God is meant to have a bearing on our lives. In this sense, God's revelation of himself is wholly practical. Always, too, the God who has 'spoken' to us has been perceived by a human mind and communicates with us in human language. Human words are time and culturally conditioned; the same is true of the human words of Scripture.

To seek to bypass the human mediator of the Word is to ignore God's way of coming to us. It is to miss the human conditioning of God's word. The ultimate 'word' of God is neither word nor text but a person – the incarnate Son. Jesus is, indeed, 'image of the invisible God' (Col 1:15). Even in this image God remains Holy Mystery because we humans see God in the limitation of the humanness of the Son.

Which God?

One would surely expect that the God we worship be, very firmly, God of the Bible. We may not fully appreciate the extent to which our traditional Christian image of God has been coloured by a concept of God that evolved within Greek philosophy. This Greek God is the unmoved mover, quite apart from the world. The Greek God is so wholly transcendent, so wholly above everything, that he cannot be immanent, that is, intimately present, in the world. God is immutable, beyond change. And God is impassible, entirely free of emotion. Our God-talk still carries much of the Greek thinking.

In contrast, the God of the Bible, the Hebrew God, is a vibrant God, geared to our humanness. The biblical writers indulged in anthropomorphism (speaking of God in human terms) and anthropopathism (attributing human emotions to God). Since the human could never be regarded as divine, there was no danger that this language would distort the difference between God and humanity. Besides, to picture God as human does not mean to think of God as human. The Hebrew God is wholly immersed in his world. The Hebrew God smiles indulgently on the wondrous richness, on the overwhelming beauty of his creation: 'It is very good'. And grieves over the suffering and sin that mar its goodness.

God of Israel

Study of the Old Testament readily discovers images of God that reflect the ambient culture. In earlier religions it was regularly assumed that the gods are easily offended by human misconduct. Angered gods punish and demand propitiation. The Hebrew God punishes but is never explicitly presented as an angry God who needs to be propitiated. Sacrifice for sin was understood not as propitiation but as expiation of sin – removal of sin. That God does punish is, indeed, the view of the prophets. The imminent Babylonian invasion was, by Jeremiah and Ezekiel, firmly presented as retribution. Post-exilic prayers of repentance candidly acknowledge guilt and the appropriateness of divine punitive action.

In an overall view of the Old Testament, however, that image of an angry God must not only be challenged but totally set aside. Our God is never God of wrath. When one reads the Old Testament as a whole one meets a prodigally loving God. This is a God not remote, aloof, but a God ever with his creation. The favoured designation of Isaiah puts it in a nutshell: the Holy One of Israel. It is a brilliant recognition of the reality of God. God is transcendent, the Holy One; God is immanent, of Israel. God is never God for God's sake. God is ever God for us.

God-for-us

The true God is God of love. God's love for us is not sentiment:

it is active and efficacious love. Our response to God's love cannot be in word only; it must be in service. And the service God looks for is our service of one another. God's love is all-embracing, but it is not possessive. His respect for humankind is tireless. He will honour human freedom.

Our response, then, should have something of the quality of God's love. It should be outgoing and delicate, sensitive to others, giving them room to grow. The way of life is the way of loving the Lord, of cleaving to him – and of being faithful to what he asks. The way of life is the way of walking in the way of God, which is the way of humanness. Who would not choose life? This life is gift – and to recognise the gift one must know the Giver. We need, more than perhaps we realise, to have a true image of God. Too many of us make do with a God who, if not a crassly false God, is not yet the God who challenges our love.

Faith in God

Because the Hebrew Bible does not really have a word for faith, what we have come to term *faith* is, in the Old Testament, described rather than defined. The description, in the main, concerns the relationship of Israel to Yahweh and the relationship to Yahweh of some key figures in Israel. In both cases the ground of faith is trust in the faithfulness of Yahweh.

At its most basic, faith is that attitude which discerns God creatively in action in the world and in human life. The perception urges the commitment of oneself in trust and obedience. The faithfulness of God denotes God's fulfilment of the obligations assumed in creating humankind and, particularly, in calling Abraham and in choosing Israel to be his people. Deuteronomy, repeatedly, makes clear that the choice had nothing to do with anything Israel was or had done. It was love alone that prompted God's call and the covenant with them that made them God's people (see Deut 4:32-40; 6:10-23). God's faithfulness was shown in delivering, saving and vindicating Israel despite Israel's own failure. God is always free. And God is not predictable – except that his *hesed*, his covenant-faithfulness, endures forever.

CHAPTER TWO

Creator

In Genesis 1 we learn that God, in whole freedom, set out to bring a universe into being, a creation with its own character and potential for development. God is Creator – the Hebrew verb *bara*, to create, is used exclusively of God. God, who is like no other, 'works' like no other. Today we recognise, in light of our understanding of the process of evolution, that the God of creation is God of *ongoing* creation. Where we spoke of God as having a *plan* for the universe, we now think of God as having a *vision*. God is God of the future. Today, we recognise that the universe, rather than being a settled phenomenon, is an open-ended adventure.

Freedom

God is God of freedom. God respects the freedom of creation through the gift of possibility. This sets up a relationship, based on freedom, between God and creation. God works from no detailed blueprint. He lets possibility be. Multiple finite freedoms are set free to explore their own possibilities and make their own way. God is God of love – and love does not manage the other. The world is not determined, cast in a fixed, inflexible mould. Nor is it undetermined, without plan or pattern of any kind. Rather, it is determinable: it can bend to circumstances. Only such a world provides scope for creaturely freedom.

This in no manner implies that God is an absentee Creator – one who created and then withdrew into Olympian aloofness. God is Creator in love with his creation. He is not 'above' creation nor 'in' creation – God is *with* his creation. This is no dominating presence but one which wholly respects and preserves creaturely freedom. It is a presence of companionship, a gracious, forgiving and saving presence. The presence of God with creation is in no sense denial of the transcendence of God or of his existence independently of creation. It does imply that God is never distant or aloof. God is present with creation in all its suffering as well as in its joy.

God, motivated by creative love, has called into being one community of creation. In our evolving world all are creatures, sustained in life by the Creator. Life on our planet began with single-cell creatures. Humble indeed, but life intent on its own development, life intrinsically involved in its own emerging forms. Humans emerged within this evolving story. We are distinctive, yes, but firmly part of this evolving world. Growth is the purpose of life; God is God of the future. God is promise and possibility. In the evolutionary process movement from one form of life to another is messy and painful. Struggle is sign of new life. Death is a necessary part of growth.

Suffering

There is much disorder in our world, so much suffering. It is a devastating fact that stands as an indictment. How can suffering on such a scale – so much innocent suffering to boot – be compatible with faith in a benevolent Creator? The question is a tormenting one. In traditional theology, God is God of order. If this be so, the question looms larger. We then have to view all that suffering – and so much disorder – as a result of divine purpose, part of a divine plan. Belief in a loving God becomes an exercise in blind faith. But, if God is a God who allows possibility and respects freedom, if creation is free from God's shaping hand, there is prospect of a more satisfying solution. Pain and suffering are not of his devising, not the consequence of a divine purpose inherent in creation.

This is as true in the natural world as in the human. Turmoil in the natural world occurs not as a feature of divinely devised aims. It is a feature of the evolutionary process. God is present, but not responsible, when a tsunami wreaks havoc, when a lion brings down its prey or when a gunman slays his victim. This because God's freedom is not separate from God's love. Traditionally, there has been more stress on the almighty power of God than on God's infinite love. It is true that God is almighty – but he does not 'throw his weight about'. He is God of might indeed, but never God of force. When one reads the Bible aright it is startlingly clear that God is, simply, God of love.

Gracious Creator

God is gracious Creator. God is not mean-minded. Today we have a perception, far beyond that of the biblical writers, of the well-nigh incredible grandeur of creation. We become more and more aware of the sheer vastness of the universe – a vastness that boggles the imagination. God has created with appropriately divine abandon. Our awe before the vast spread of the universe leads to awe of the Creator. God's creative deed is free. God had, absolutely, no need of the universe, no need of humankind. But he did bring us into being.

As a result, one can say, with truth, that humankind is necessary to God – necessary in the sense that deed of God has to be meaningful. Creation was not a whim. God was in deadly earnest. There lies our hope, our assurance. God has made us for himself, has called us to be his children. God waits for our response. God needs us, needs us to know our need of him. A lesser God would have made a better job of it! He would have created beings who could not but acknowledge their dependence and be wholly thankful to their Creator. Our God has no time for slaves. His only weapon is love. His children will be freely his children. Only a God who is God would call into being creatures who might say No! to their Creator.

God is Creator of a universe. While we humans, with God's help, discern our place in his purpose, we have tended to be self-centred. Have we not been prone to regard ourselves as in some sort, focus of God's well-nigh exclusive attention? And, in our tiny corner of this vast world, we have acted, and do act, as though all else on our planet were solely for our use and benefit. We need a humbler view, a more realistic view. Humility is truth.

Humankind

'Let us make humankind in our image, according to our likeness' (Gen 21:16). This is the high moment of the primeval creation story of Genesis. Image of God refers to the characteristics that make communication with God possible and that enable humans to undertake God-given responsibilities. It is significant that the Hebrew word *ha-adam* is humankind male *and* female – 'in the image of God he created them' (1:27): the female images the divine as fully as does the male. Likeness to God is found in what is distinctive to man and woman as well as in what they share.

Today we realise that Earth is but one planet in our galaxy, that it is but a speck in a vast universe. There may be creatures in other worlds with whom the Creator may communicate. We do not know. We do know that, in our world, with humans alone can God dialogue. Despite the different realities of divine and human this dialogue will be free. God is God of freedom who has made us free and meticulously respects our freedom Often one hears the complaint: if God be God, why is our world in such a mess – a mess largely of our making! Why does God not take steps to clean up the mess? The answer lies in God's respect for our freedom. God might wave a magic wand. The cost is too high – the sacrifice of freedom – and he will not exact the price. God might have programmed our world. But he does not choose to converse with robots.

Humankind is God's image in another respect: his representative who will administer the earth in God's name. 'Have dominion': God has designated responsibility. It is unfortunate – disastrous indeed – that dominion was to become the primary model for the relation between humans and the natural world. In fact, in the Bible, it is highlighted only in Genesis and Psalm 8.

In truth, humankind has been granted no licence to exploit – in a destructive sense – nature, to despoil the earth. Pope Francis has expressed this forthrightly: 'if we Christians have at times incorrectly interpreted the Scriptures, nowadays we must forcefully reject the notion that our being created in God's image and given dominion over the earth justifies absolute domination over other creatures' (*Laudato Si'*, 67).

Humankind's special obligation, as image of God, is one of respect for the natural world. God has concern for all his creation, not only for humankind. If humans are unfaithful in their stewardship, which, because it is humanly gifted, will be creative, they not only fail the Creator but betray the earth.

To be like God

Humankind receives a command: ' ... of the tree of knowledge of good and evil you shall not eat' (Gen 2:16-17). Law is impersonal; a command sets up a relationship. The command is an acknowledgment of human freedom. Humans can obey or disobey. The temptation story (Gen 3) brings matters to a head. The function of the *nahash,* a talking snake – a stage-prop – is to focus attention on the command and to spell out disobedience as, in effect, a vain attempt 'to be like God'. It will remain the perennial human temptation.

This is graphically presented in the Babel story (Gen 11:1-9). It, too, is a story of disobedience. The divine charge to human-kind to fill the earth and assume responsibility in furthering God's purpose for his creation (2:28), repeated after the flood (9:1), is being challenged. The people of Babel seek to shelter themselves from the 'scattering'. They seek to secure their future.: 'Let us build ourselves a city ... let us make a name for ourselves; otherwise we will be scattered abroad' (11:4). Not alone is the divine charge ignored, these people seek to live independently of God: let *us* build ... let *us* make a name for ourselves. They are 'being like God'.

The 'primal' sin is found in the fact that humans, in one fashion or another, do not want to acknowledge their own finitude. This is because finitude is regarded as flaw rather than regarded for what it is: a necessary and inescapable feature of our creaturehood. It is human destiny to be human beings in a real world, a world that is wondrous but is also a world of failure and of suffering. The finitude of the world and of hu-manity is not the result of a fall from grace. Our belief in God as Creator does not deny the finitude of creation, nor does it distort contingency into sin or fallenness. God abides with the contingent, that is to say, with the world in its limitation and with humankind in its finite humanity. Human greatness is with God, never apart from God, because it must be within the realm of creaturehood. 'To be like God' is vain, and always disastrous.

—

CHAPTER THREE

Parent

The God of the Bible, the Father of our Lord Jesus Christ, is the foolish God (see 1 Cor 1:18-21). What Paul has declared of the paradox of the Cross – that, though scandal to Jews and foolishness to Gentiles, it is, in truth, the power and wisdom of God – may be extended to the whole saving plan of God. Indeed, 'God's foolishness is wiser than human wisdom'. God's gamble was in making us free. He stands, stolidly, by that gamble. God is, happily, not an Unmoved Mover. God is not only Creator. God is Parent. Our human grace is not that we are creatures of God, not even that we are image of God. The ultimate divine foolishness, made emphatic in Christian revelation, is that we are children of God (see Romans 8:14-17; 1 John 3:1-2). This is Christian truth – but it must reach to all of humanity.

Parent

Traditionally, our God is Father. Our God-language, including the God-language of Scripture, is emphatically male. Our God-image is andromorphic – male-imaged. Because the Bible itself comes out of and reflects a patriarchal culture, it tends to be androcentric, male-centred. The predominant biblical images for God are taken from male experience, with God being depicted as Father, King, Warrior and so on. At the same time there is an intriguing openness to female imagery, with God being imaged as birth-giving woman and loving mother (see Deut 33:18; Is42:14; 66:13). In point of fact, it makes as much sense to refer to God as Mother as it does to call God 'Father'. God is neither male nor female; God stands apart from such categories – God is transcendent, wholly above and beyond created reality.

To call God 'Father' is to acknowledge that God is the source of our being, of our life, in a measure that is, in some fashion, comparable to our parents' role: they bring us into being and care for us. In that sense, God is Parent. But we do not know what divine 'parenthood' might mean – except that it must outstrip, infinitely, in graciousness the most lovable human parental relationship. Indeed, at its best, human parental love can be a thing of wonder. For instance, there is the self-sacrificing loving care of a severely-handicapped child. It is by bringing together father-love and mother-love that we arrive at the fullness of parental love. In view of this, surely 'parent' is the term most appropriate to convey an inkling of divine love. God is parent. And just there is divine vulnerability. What loving parent can ever, ever reject the child. There is the comforting assurance of Isaiah 49:15:

> Can a woman forget her nursing child
> or show contempt for the child of her womb?
> Even these may forget,
> yet I will never forget you.

Jesus addressed God as Father – indeed, more intimately as *Abba*. He thereby expressed their relationship in the conventional language of his historical humanness. This tells us not only of his personal relationship with God but of the rich meaning of fatherhood in his Hebrew tradition.. But the use of the term 'father', even by Jesus, does not mean that God is, in any sense, male. Appreciation of analogical language reminds us that we do not really know what it really means for God to be 'Parent'. It surely does not mean that God is male – or female for that matter.

Children of God

'Beloved, we are God's children now; what we will be has yet to be revealed' (1 Jn 3:2). The New Testament assures us that our God looks upon us humans as his children. But that was the divine intent from the first. God might have been a benevolent Creator with a benign regard for his human creatures. But our God seeks a closer relationship: he would be Parent. The Parent soon discovers that these children are problem children: 'Children have I reared and brought up, but they have rebelled against me' (Is 1:2).

The story of the Flood (Gen 6-9) is of major religious significance. It dramatizes the destructive nature of sin and the reaction of God to sin. As with all biblical stories, it is essential to put the right question: What does it mean? Throughout the Flood story we are in the presence of myth: an expression of universal truth in symbolic terms. It is a paradigm of an ongoing biblical concern. God represents infinite love and mercy and forgiveness. He wills the salvation of all. But how is one to portray the divinely loving forgiveness of God without conveying the false impression that he shrugs off sin as incidental? The Flood story is an attempt to do this.

The significance of the answer comes to light in a startling reprise: the repeated statement in the introduction and conclusion of the story. At the beginning: 'every inclination of the thoughts of their hearts was only evil continually' (6:5). At the close, after the promise that there will never be another flood, a similar observation: 'for the inclination of the human heart is evil from youth' (8:21). The comfort: God has decided to bear with humankind's tendency to evil. There is our comfort: this foolish God is determined to put up with his wayward children. Edward Schillebeeckx aptly characterises creation, and notably creation of humankind, as a divine adventure full of risks:

> By giving creative space to human beings, God makes himself vulnerable. It is an adventure full of risks... The creation of human beings is a blank cheque for which God alone is guarantor. By creating human beings with their own finite and free will, God voluntarily renounces power. That makes him to a high degree dependent on human beings and thus vulnerable. (*Church: The Human Story of God*)

We are reminded of a remarkable episode in Genesis 18. God had decided that he must take action against the wickedness of Sodom and Gomorrah. But he feels he must first brief Abraham: 'Shall I hide from Abraham what I am about to do ... for I have chosen him?' (18:17-19). Abraham, for his part, is flabbergasted. The Lord had not thought the matter through; surely he is not planning to wipe out the righteous! 'Far be it from you to do such a thing, to slay the righteous with the wicked ... shall not the Judge of all the earth do what is just?' (18:24-26). This is putting it up to God and no mistake. And, having made his point, Abraham pleads for the people of Sodom. We catch the flavour of a bargaining bout in an oriental bazaar with prices being ruthlessly slashed: 45, 40, 30, 10. He realises that lower than ten righteous persons he cannot go. But he had had a valiant try.

That the author of this story could, in such an uninhibited manner, present this lively dialogue between a human and God reveals a profound appreciation of God. He is a transcendent God. But he is not a remote God. And surely not a fearsome

God. He has a sense of humour. He plays along with Abraham. He is a God who displays respect for humankind.

Sadly, in the Flood story, God had come to observe that the thoughts and inclinations of humans are perverse. Yet he was determined that 'never again shall there be a flood to destroy the earth'. Humankind has not changed. God has changed. God's purpose had been resisted. His decision is to live with this resistance. But God is not resigned to live with evil. He has made a promise – a covenant: 'I will establish my covenant with you, that never again shall there be a flood to destroy the earth' (9:11). This is God's own self-limitation on his reaction to sin, to human spurning of him. The rebellion of humankind had grieved God to his heart. God will continue to grieve. God has created humankind in his image. Sinful humans remain in the image of God (9:6), they retain dominion over God's world. It is, however, a world now touched by their sinfulness (9:2-3; see Rom 8:18-25). They still have responsibility for the created order. Humans will continue to fail, but not because creation has failed. And, somehow, God will have the last word.

We are left with the problem of evil and sin. We cannot accept that God is unconcerned. We feel, however, that there has to be a balance to the strange mercy of our God. So, there is the notion of the 'wrath' of God. The idea of God oscillating between wrath and mercy is a misguided human attempt to find balance where, in divine terms, there is no balance to be struck. We ask the question: How may one reconcile God's mercy with God's justice? It is a mistaken question. The first Christian theologian (Paul) got the matter right: 'Has not God made foolish the wisdom of the world? ... God's foolishness is wiser than human wisdom' (1 Cor 1:20, 25).

Too many later theologians have misunderstood. Let us settle for a foolish God The comfort: this foolish God is determined to put up with his wayward children. Sadly, God would come to observe that the thoughts and inclinations of humans are perverse. Yet he has determined that 'never again shall there be a flood to destroy the earth'. God will have the last word. He will because he is God of salvation and human salvation is all about being truly human. And that means becoming truly a child of God.

Israel

Our Parent desires dialogue with his children. In furthering his plan of salvation for sinful humanity, he chose and called one human community to be his special people, to, bear witness to him. The call was marked by promise and was sealed by covenant: 'I am your God; you are my people'. The people of Israel proved unfaithful. Their God remained constant and faithful.

The God of the Old Testament is the Holy One of Israel, a God transcendent and immanent. One might term the Old Testament the book of Two Constancies. There is the constancy of human unfaithfulness, documented with refreshing candour. And there is the accompanying, and prevailing, constancy of divine faithfulness. God will be faithful – no matter what. Indeed, one senses a gut feeling: Israel's innate persuasion that God, having freely chosen Israel, is stuck with Israel. It is surely the conviction of that proud Israelite, Paul: 'God has not rejected his people whom he foreknew' – because 'the gifts and calling of God are irrevocable' (Rom 11: 2, 29).

CHAPTER FOUR

Just and Merciful God

Just God

When we speak of God we must keep in mind that no human expression can be taken literally. This because we cannot know God in God's own self. I can say, with truth, that God is a loving God; I speak out of my experience of human love. My assertion is not meaningless, though I can have but an inkling of the reality of divine love.

It is when we turn to justice that we can go hopelessly wrong. The error is when what reasonably operates as justice on the human level is taken to be operative in the world of God. Consider this statement: 'God is a just God who deals with us fairly'. By human standards, fine. But does any of us wish to be treated *fairly* by God? Do we wish God to deal with us as we truly deserve? Surely we hope to be treated with loving mercy. And that is how our just God does treat us – because divine justice is mercy. We need to look to the biblical under-standing of justice.

Justice

The central fact of Exodus was the freeing of Hebrew slaves from Egyptian bondage. The contest with Pharaoh shows a God committed to establishming justice in a regime organised against justice. It is noteworthy that Yahweh acted in response to the suffering of slaves:

> The Israelites groaned under their slavery and cried out...

God heard their groaning... God looked upon the Israel-ites and God took notice of them (Ex 2:22-23).

I have observed the misery of my people who are in Egypt... I know their suffering and I have come down to deliver them (3: 7-8).

In this matter of justice it is essential to be quite clear that what is at issue is *distributive* justice. This means the distribution of social goods and the sharing of power. It is the awareness that the wellbeing of a community requires that possessions be, to an extent, given up by the wealthy for the sake of those who do not have enough, and power tempered by the power-ful in favour of the powerless. Israel understood that such was a demand of Yahweh. His passion for justice is meant to be implemented concretely in human practice.

We are more familiar with a different concept of justice: *retributive* justice. It means giving to persons what is their just desert on the basis of performance. So, for instance, the notion of a just wage and of punishment of misconduct – in general, a system of reward and punishment. While retributive justice was indeed recognised in Israel, emphasis is, undoubtedly, on distributive justice. This is not to say that the consequent obligation was always , or predominantly, carried through in practice. In Israel, as in every society, there was tension between 'haves' and 'have-nots'.

But there can be little doubt that the advocates of distribu-tive justice occupy the central space in the testimony of Israel. Remarkable across the different Old Testament traditions is an insistence on the obligation to care for those too weak to protect themselves. There is the principle expressed in Deu-teronomy 15:11:

Since there will never cease to be some in need on the

earth, I therefore command you, 'Open your hand to the poor and needy neighbour in your land'.

That there will always be poor is realistic acknowledgment of our sinful human situation. It is no fatalistic acceptance. It is challenge.

God as Judge

In practice, this biblical preoccupation with distributive justice has been downplayed or ignored. And the justice of God has been heard as retributive justice. Consequently, God has been cast as a Judge who, along the line of retributive justice, hands out reward and punishment. We speak glibly of God as a just Judge. Well it is for us that God is unjust! We have tended to categorise sin as crime. So, we 'break' the commandments. We commonly referred to the sacrament of reconciliation as the 'tribunal' of penance. In this setting a repentant sinner is a criminal appearing before a judge. Very well – what happens? If God be Judge, he is a Judge who acquits the guilty – one who enters a plea of guilty – the repentant sinner. It is not a matter of handing down a lenient sentence or a suspended sentence. No; the judge simply accepts the plea of guilty (acknowledgment of sin), and dismisses the case (forgiveness). A human judge who would act so could not expect to hold his job for long. But God is doing it all the time.

We should rejoice in the *injustice* of our God. Indeed, we might question the propriety of imaging God as judge at all. *We* seem to have a problem in our striving to reconcile God's mercy with justice. Let us not lose any sleep over it: *God* has no such problem.

God has given voice to his pain at his people's rejection of him, his sorrow that the people, by and large, had gone astray.

Israel was his people: I am your God, you are my people. He had established a covenant with his people – 'my covenant which you broke'. They had spurned him, had gone their own way. Their stubbornness could not wear him down.

Paul had understood when, against all logic, he maintained: 'all Israel will be saved.' Why? 'Because the gifts and the call of God are irrevocable' (Rom 11:36, 29). There is the comfort for humans. All are called to be children of God. He is faithful though all prove unfaithful. He is ever Parent, though we be fickle children.

Compassion

Our traditional God is an aloof figure – often a forbidding figure. Strangely, while he is firmly presented as one gravely offended by human sin, he is made to appear unaffected by human suffering. But biblical metaphor demands that we acknowledge a God who grieves and laments and suffers. God is God of compassion – he suffers with his suffering children. Pain and woe are not of his devising.. Pain is of the web and woof of human life, not a punishment imposed on humankind. Pain and death are part of our evolutionary world – not only of the human world. Why? Today we recognise this to be a necessary feature of the evolutionary process. To view pain and death as punishment inflicted by a 'just' God is to demean God. But it has been the way of religious tradition. We honour God by accepting our human lot as challenge, challenge to look above and raise our eyes beyond pain and mortality. We are helped, immeasurably, if we look to a God of compassion who is with us in our woe and in our death.

Strangest of all, most comforting of all, God bears the burden of human sin. That is God's decision after the Flood (Gen

8:21). He is wearied by human sin; he bears with it. Birth, new life, comes out of pain. God is pregnant with life, Mother of new creation.

There is one answer only to the evil that is sin – and to all evil. Violence can never be the answer. Nothing but love, the infinitely patient divine love, can absorb evil and put it out of commission. God does not suffer in silence. He protests against any manipulation of him. But he suffers – in the manner in which *God* may suffer. He feels and shares the pain inflicted in his name on the weak and vulnerable. So many have been broken, so many have been shattered, in the name of God. Throughout history, to our day, God has been dishonoured. He has been wearied, beyond measure. Because too often and with frightening consistency, religious observance has been denial of, or suppression of, human values. Any depreciation of human values is denial of the God of humankind.

The language of suffering – analogical, of course – is an essential ingredient of a balanced portrait of God. It adds, immeasurably, to his attractiveness and counters, effectively, many false 'gods' of our religious heritage. There is, surely, something compelling about a God who grieves for humankind gone astray. A God who suffers because of his people's rejection of him, who suffers with his suffering people, is, indeed, a challenging God. He is, surely, the foolish God discerned by Paul. He is the God who has shown that he is not aloof from pain and sorrow and death. He is the kind of God we need. He is *our* God.

Merciful God

Our tendency is to limit the reach of God's love. Sadly, a loving Parent suffers misunderstanding and ingratitude. There is even scandal at the Parent's mercy to sinners. There seems to be a rooted reluctance to acknowledge and wholeheartedly welcome a gracious God – in particular when that graciousness is directed to others.

Reluctant Prophet

The story of Jonah – a brilliantly satirical short story – mounts a protest. It tells of a reluctant prophet sent with a message of warning to Nineveh, capital of the Assyrian empire and symbol of oppression. Nineveh was in modern Iraq, very definitely to the east of Palestine; Jonah headed west – 'away from the presence of the Lord'. He feared that mercy and forgiveness might lurk within the word of threat. His worst fears were realised. God relented and spared the repentant Ninevites (Jon 3:10). 'But this was very displeasing to Jonah' (4:1).

The tragedy of his stance is caught up in one astonishing statement:

> He prayed to the Lord and said, 'O Lord! This is why I fled to the west at the beginning: for I knew that you are a gracious God and merciful, slow to anger, and abounding in steadfast love' (4:2-3).

Jonah had fled his God. That was grave indeed. The enormity is that he had fled *this* God – a God gracious, merciful, of steadfast love. There is the rub: infinite love, a love that knew no limit, no frontier. This was too much. It is all too reminiscent of the reaction to the word and praxis of Jesus: 'This fellow welcomes sinners and eats with them! (Lk 15:2). It is never easy for the 'righteous' to come to terms with an 'unjust' God. Jonah, then, underlines the predictable human reaction to divine generosity. If my God is gracious to me –

fine. He dare not be gracious to those whom we have judged to be undeserving of his mercy.

Wrath

The prophets Of Israel proposed no theory of God, did not seek to expound the nature of God. They offered instead God's understanding of humankind and his concern for humanity. Very particularly, they had an insight into the *pathos* of God — the Greek term refers to experience, to being intrinsically affected by events or persons. Pathos is not an attribute of God. It is an expression of God's loving care for his creation; it marks a God involved in history.

The fundamental concern of the Bible is not creation but God's care for creation. The basic feature of pathos is divine attentiveness and concern. Above all, it is the divine attentiveness to humanity. Indeed, it is through his pathos, his relation to Israel and to humanity, that we can know God at all. We can think of God only insofar as God thinks of us. God thinks of us always with concern. The dominant pathos of God is love or mercy. But there is also the pathos of wrath.

It is undeniable that Scripture does speak of the 'wrath' of God. God's 'anger' is an aspect of divine pathos; it is so as response to human sin. The biblical term 'anger' denotes what we call righteous indignation. It is impatience with evil. Psalm 7:11 puts it like this: 'God is a righteous judge, and a God who has indignation every day'. In the Bible, a judge is not only a person competent to consider a case and pronounce sentence, but one who is pained and distressed by injustice.

The pathos of anger is never regarded as an attribute of God, but as a response of God. In its origin and in its duration it is clearly distinguished from mercy. This is beautifully expressed

—

in Isaiah 54:7-8:

> For a brief moment I abandoned you,
> but with great compassion I will gather you.
> In overflowing wrath for a moment I hid my face from
> you,
> but with everlasting love I will have compassion on
> you,
> says the Lord your Redeemer.

'Brief moment' – 'great compassion'; wrath 'for a moment' – 'everlasting love': there is a radical inbalance. Compassion flows from the love of a Redeemer. 'Wrath' is the grieving of a spurned Parent. There is a biblical belief in divine grace, divine compassion. There is no belief in abiding and consuming divine anger. What is often proclaimed of love, famously in the refrain of Psalm 136 – 'for his steadfast love endures forever' – is never said about anger. The normal and original pathos is love, mercy.

Repentance

Sin is a reality. When one is conscious of having failed, and having failed dismally, what does one do? This was the situation of those who suffered the sixth century BCE Babylonian exile. The faith answer to the disaster was repentance and hope. The people had failed – of that there could be no doubt. But Yahweh was steadfast as ever. There was a way of restoration, a way of redemption. It was the way of candid confession of sin and of total trust in God's boundless mercy.

The many moving prayers to be found in Baruch, Ezra and Nehemiah, Tobit, Sirach Esther, Judith and the Book of Daniel follow this way. We may find encouragement and comfort in these prayers. They are straightforward: we have sinned; we deserve all that has come upon us. Are we depressed? No! We acknowledge our sin, our shameful ingratitude – and we turn to God. We have sinned, we have failed – but you are You! It is, in some sort, an anticipation of: 'I shall arise and go to my Father'.

While post-exilic prayers tend to be lengthy, there is about them a refreshing candour and an inspiring faith. They are the prayers of a chastened people, a people that, in adversity, had found its soul. Those who pray confess sin openly. They do not grovel, but maintain a quiet dignity. Most instructive is a recurring phrase that characterises God as 'the great and awesome God who keeps covenant and steadfast love with those who love him' – followed always by the confession: 'We have sinned'. Those who pray these prayers have discovered the way of restoration, the way of redemption.

Post-exilic Prayers

Baruch 1:15–3:8
Ezra 9:6-18
Nehemiah 1:5-11; 9:6-37
Tobit 13:1-8
Sirach 36:1-17
Esther 13:9-17; 14:3-19
Judith 9:2-14
Daniel 3:26-45; 9:4-19].

CHAPTER FIVE

Saviour – Redeemer

The great sixth-century BCE prophet, whom we call Second Isaiah (author of Isaiah 40-55) stressed belief in God as Creator. More distinctively, he presented this Creator God as Redeemer and Saviour. These related titles are prominent in his text. Two instances:

> For your Maker is your husband, the Lord of hosts is his name; the Holy One of Israel is your Redeemer (Is 54:5).

> I am the Lord your God, the Holy One of Israel, your Saviour (43:3).

Like the titles, the notions of redemption and salvation are related.

Redemption

The term 'redeem' refers to what was originally a practice in Israelite family law. One might have surrendered a piece of family property to settle a debt. Or, more seriously, one might have entered into service as a slave to work off a debt. In such circumstances, the next of kin had a legal obligation to redeem the debt in order to regain the property or win the freedom of the one enslaved. The one who did this was a 'redeemer' -- *goel* in Hebrew. See Leviticus 25:25. For an individual to be so redeemed meant to be liberated from the hands of outsiders and restored to the family circle. In Exodus we read that, in relation to the enslaved Israelites, Yahweh assumed this responsibility.

I have heard the groaning of the Israelites, whom the Egyptians are holding as slaves ... I am the Lord and I will deliver you from the burdens of the Egyptians and deliver you from slavery to them. I will redeem you ... I will take you as my people, and I will be your God. You shall know that I am the Lord your God who has freed you from the burdens of the Egyptians (Ex 6:5-7).

The idea of God as Redeemer (*goel*) became firmly fixed in Israelite religious tradition. As did the related titles, Redeemer, Saviour. Eventually, the conviction would acquire universal resonance: humanity, enslaved to sin, alienated from God, restored to the family of God. This is the deed of a compassionate God, motivated by love.

Forgiveness

God is gracious, but his children have been less than gracious. Sin is pervasive. We stand in need of forgiveness. We must open our hearts to a forgiveness that is freely offered – to be received in freedom. We must turn to our Parent. To seek God's forgiveness is a homecoming; to be forgiven is to be welcomed home.

In our human experience, forgiveness does not come lightly. An offence is all the more hurtful when it is inflicted by one near and dear. In our human manner, we think it reasonable that forgiveness be shrouded in conditions; we exact reparation of some sort. This is not to suggest that forgiveness may not be wholehearted and sincere. It is simply not easy for us to ignore a deep hurt. The reminder of it is within us, in our very being.

From what we have so far seen of God, it ought not surprise us that God is emphatically a God of forgiveness. Yet, one of the things about God which humans find hard to accept is the breadth and depth of God's forgiveness. When we temper the forgiveness of God by the standard of our forgiveness we get it wrong. Indeed, consistent with our often flawed image of God we assume that such forgiveness is grudging: an offended deity is prepared to forgive, provided he gets his pound of flesh. It is a sad travesty of God's forgiveness. Yet it is one that is prevalent.

The robust faith of the prophets may bring encouragement. Isaiah carries a prayer attributed to king Hezekiah after he had been snatched from the brink of death. It has the hopeful word: 'it was for my welfare that I had great bitterness ... for you have cast all my sins behind your back' (Is 38:17). Micah, in his lament for Zion, declares: 'Who is a God like you, pardoning iniquity, and passing over transgressions? He will again have compassion upon us. He will tread our iniquities under foot. You will cast all our sins into the depths of the sea' (Mic 7:18-19). What powerful images! What mighty consolation! 'You have cast all my sins behind your back'; you have snatched them from me, thrown them over your shoulder, and have walked on, without a backward glance. 'He will tread our iniquities under foot'; he will cover them over, deeply and firmly, will bury them forever from his sight. 'You will cast all my sins into the depths of the sea'; you will lift the crushing burdens that wear us down and sink them in the murky depths where such dark things belong.

This is the prophets' image of divine forgiveness, worthy of their God. Only Jesus could do better with his picture of the loving Father who, without question and without condition, welcomes and reinstates the errant son (Lk 15:20-24).

A practical way of approaching the truth of God's forgiveness is in the context of the sacrament of Reconciliation. A seemingly forgotten truth is that God's forgiveness is sheer gift: unearned and unmerited. Though we speak of the gift of God's forgiveness, many feel that they must earn it. The reality is that the initiative comes from God. This has been expressed forthrightly by theologian Herbert McCabe:

> Never be deluded into thinking that if you have contrition, if you are sorry for your sins, God will come and forgive you – that he will be touched by your appeal, change his mind about you and forgive you. Not a bit of it. God never changes his mind about you. What he does, again and again, is change your mind about him. That is why you are sorry. That is what your forgiveness is. You are not forgiven because you confess your sin. You confess your sin, recognise yourself for what you are, because you are forgiven. (*Faith within Reason*)

There remains the central reality of forgiveness. Too often, God's deed is set in a grim context of reparation that strips it of its graciousness. What ought to follow on forgiveness is loving response. Luke touchingly reveals this in his story of 'a woman in the city who was a sinner' (Lk 7:36-50). She was a woman who had previously encountered Jesus and had received his forgiveness. She made a brave and extravagant gesture: she kissed the feet of a reclining Jesus, to the manifest scandal of his Pharisee host. Jesus accepted her presence and ministering with gentle courtesy. His verdict was clear and to the point: 'Her great love proves that her sins have been forgiven' (v. 47) One is not casual in face of forgiveness. But one's response is not in 'making up' to an offended deity.

The best way of responding to forgiveness is by extending forgiveness to others. In Matthew's parable of The Unmerciful Servant (Mt 18:13-35) we meet again the sinner and his God. An impossible debt is casually written off in response to the sinner's plea, but when the recipient of such forgiveness cannot find it in his heart to be merciful, the master is 'angry' (18:33).

Response to God's gracious forgiveness cannot be payment of a debt that is already fully remitted. It is, instead, warm thanks given for the blessing of such forgiving love. And readiness to be forgiving in our turn.

Salvation

A yearning for salvation is a profoundly human desire. It is, in one form or other, at the core of every religion. We humans know ourselves to be flawed. We set goals before ourselves and fail to reach them. Time and again we find, to our dismay, that we are more frail than we had feared. We may seek to fool ourselves but cannot sustain the deception. We are unwhole but long for wholeness. We look for salvation.

What is salvation? It is perceived in various ways; it has been made to mean many things. It has been made to seem ethereal, unreal. It has been presented as transcending humanness, even as denying humanness. This is tragic because salvation means nothing other than attaining perfect humanness. To put it simply: each of us is a human being – but we are flawed human beings. Our destiny is to be wholly human – as God understands humanness. When I have reached that goal I have become what I am meant to be: I am saved. To put it more theologically: we are human beings, created in the image of God. We are meant to *image* God – in our humanness.

Salvation happens in our world, in our history. Salvation comes from God but happens, as it must, in the lives of human beings. It reaches into and touches every aspect of human life. Otherwise it would not be salvation of humankind. Salvation is not confined within the limits of religion. Indeed, too often religion has been and is an obstacle to salvation – the whole revelation of the wholly human. And it is only when men and women are free to be truly human that the human person becomes image of God. It is only so that the true being of God may be revealed. Revelation of God occurs where doing good brings about liberation, breaking the bonds that stifle whatever is truly human.

God is most unambiguously revealed in human love. This accounts for the New Testament emphasis on love of one another, love even of the enemy. None of this is pie-in-the-sky. Our faith experience of redemption is lived out in finitude, in conditions that are not at all evidently redeemed. We are theoretically unable to reconcile the reality of redemption from sin and death with actual human suffering, with the troubled state of our world. Hope-filled faith is the response to the situation. Faith does not spare us the darkness and the riddle, but it is the answer as it reaches, through the darkness and beyond the riddle, to the Son and to the Father.

We are conscious of struggle in our world. We experience struggle within ourselves. We imagine that God and evil are locked in combat. Nothing in our world would assure us that, in the last resort, good, not evil, will triumph. Faith in a benevolent Creator offers the only – and certain – assurance. The finitude of our existence is caught up in his world of creation. We are meant to be human beings in a sphere that is, simply, the world. It is futile to look for salvation outside our creaturely existence.

Christian salvation is salvation of and for human beings – men and women of flesh and blood. The goal of salvation, in our present world, is the creation of a free society for free human beings. This is what is meant by 'kingdom of God', better, rule of God. Salvation is not, nor was it ever meant to be, salvation of 'souls'. It is a matter of healing, of making whole, the person. It includes and involves society and the world of nature. It comprises eschatological, social and political aspects. The process of salvation means that, here and now, we strive to be human, in our mortality and in our suffering. If this is not so, then Jesus of, Nazareth is not the *whole* human being that our faith acknowledges him to be. And, as we shall see, Jesus in his ministry was always concerned with *people*. He brought comfort to sinners indeed. But he healed the sick and he comforted the afflicted and the outcasts. He was not in the business of saving 'souls'.

CHAPTER SIX

Image of the Invisible God

Up to now, we have been considering aspects of our God as presented in the Old Testament. Now we look to the uniquely Christian presentation of this God in New Testament revelation.

God in a new light

Our God is Father of our Lord Jesus Christ, who has shown himself in the life and cross of Jesus of Nazareth. God is truly the God of the Old Testament whom Jesus addressed as *Abba* – Father, with familiar resonance. The difference is that, through revelation by the Son, we perceive God more clearly.

The New Testament brings more sharply and emphatically before us a concerned and caring Parent: 'God so loved the world that he gave his only Son' (Jn 3:16), and gave himself in the giving. We measure love by our human experience of love. If we strive to measure divine love we need to think the unthinkable, believe the unbelievable. God has revealed himself to us in the human person, in the life, death and resurrection of Jesus of Nazareth. In him, God has come to walk with us. In him, God has suffered among us and at our hands. It is always the same God, from the first page of the Bible to the last. We Christians find this God in the Son.

The Son

'Who do you say that I am?' (Mk 8:29). This challenging

question put to the disciples at Caesarea Philippi is one that Christians have continued to answer over the centuries. It may be argued that the earliest answers are still the best. One looks to Paul. His response rings with conviction: Jesus is 'the image of the invisible God' (Col 1:15).

The Fourth Gospel offers a relevant commentary: 'No one has ever seen God. It is God the only Son, who is close to the Father's heart, who has made him known' (Jn 1:18). The transcendent unknowable God is now visible and knowable in the Son: 'the Word became flesh and lived among us' (1:14). And, throughout the Fourth Gospel, the role of the Son is Revealer of the Father.

The author of Hebrews makes his contribution: 'Long ago God spoke to our ancestors in many and various ways by the prophets, but in these last days he has spoken to us by a Son … he is the reflection of God's glory and the exact imprint of God's very being' (Heb 1:1-3). God had indeed spoken in the Scriptures of Israel and continues to speak to us there. But now there is, besides, a definitive word, a word not uttered or written, a word that is *person*, the Son. Put more simply, Jesus of Nazareth is the human person in whom God is wholly present. For, if Jesus is image of the invisible God, he is so as a human person, like us in all things. *Jesus* tells us what God is like, *Jesus* is God's summons to us, God's challenge to us.

God-for-us

'God was in Christ, reconciling the world to himself' (2 Cor 5:19). This is, arguably, the very best christological statement, and it weds Christology, the theological understanding of Jesus Christ, with the theology of salvation, soteriology. Where Jesus is, there is God, and God is God *for us*. But Jesus of Nazareth was 'born of woman' (Gal 4:4), lived in our world, and died, horribly, on a cross. We cannot know God in God's own self. But we can know God in this Jesus. Jesus tells us what God is like. We can say, truly, that God is love; we have no idea what divine love is in itself. In Jesus, we see God's love in action. We learn that God is God who is with us in our suffering and at our death. We are sure of it because of the suffering and death of Jesus.

In Jesus, God has shown himself in human form: 'He is the image of the invisible God'. In practice, we have slipped quickly past this human aspect. We have turned, instead, to a 'divine icon' comfortably free of any trait of the critical prophet. We had consigned Jesus to his heavenly home. And wisely, because we had realised a long time ago that he is safer there! We genuflect before 'our divine Lord' who does not impinge on us because of the manner in which we envisage him. He does not really have any critical impact on the life of our world. But Jesus of Nazareth is a very uncomfortable person to have about. There remains the Gospel and its challenge, its 'dangerous memory'.

The Way

We cannot but believe that the first Christians had an understanding of Jesus sharpened by their very nearness to 'the things that have happened in these days ... concerning Jesus of Nazareth' (Lk 24:18-19) – an understanding that, for us, has been blunted by a weight of theology, not always helpful. It is not easy for us to fight our way through to Jesus of Nazareth. It is essential that we strive.

We do want to make our way to God. What we must learn to accept is that God has first made his way to us. The first sin was humanity's snatching at the wisdom that can only be theirs as gift (Gen 3:1-7). Humanity's sin continues to be its striving to escape the ways of God. It has long perturbed me that Old Testament men and women often had a better understanding of God and, certainly, a more personal relationship with God, than is the experience of many Christians. In Jesus of Nazareth the divine has entered into our world, our history. God has become one with us. But we would bypass the way of God. The basic Christian truth is: 'I am the Way' (Jn 14:6). If God's way to humankind is through the man Jesus, then our way to God is through the man Jesus.

I have stressed the *man* Jesus. Is Jesus not God? I would suggest that the statement 'Jesus is God' effectively blunts the challenge of Jesus. To say 'Jesus is God' implies not only that we know who Jesus is – but that we know who and what God is. It is Jesus who reveals God to us. 'To argue from God to Jesus instead of arguing from Jesus to God is to put the cart before the horse' – as Albert Nolan puts it in *Jesus before Christianity*. Jesus the man of flesh and blood shows us the true image of God whom we find to be, paradoxically, a *Deus humanissimus* – a supremely human God – this Father of our Lord Jesus Christ.

But we can see him only if we allow Jesus of Nazareth to be human. This Jesus is, indeed, Emmanuel, he is God-with-us. We are faced with mystery here. How is one to speak of this unique meeting of God with humanity, this union of divinity and humanness, in terms that will not betray one or the other aspect of the mystery? Scripture has come up with 'Father' and 'Son'. We must be grateful for this and live with the mystery.

To diminish the human reality of Jesus is to screen from sight the God who would shine through him. There is a style of Christology that has tended to do just that. It has done so because it has been so influenced by the image of a distant

Greek God, apart from humanity. Instead, we need to acknowledge a vulnerable Jesus if we are to meet our vulnerable God. The mystery of Jesus is that in him God reveals himself in a manner that speaks to our humanness. Jesus' divinity is not, as sometimes presented, a kind of second substance in him. His divinity consists in the fact that, as the perfect counterpart of God, he is the manifestation and presence of God in our world. Any misrepresentation that 'Jesus is human, but...' – and it is all too common – is, effectively, refusal of the God who revealed himself in Jesus.

When the human Jesus is not acknowledged, our understanding of God suffers and our Christianity suffers. Edward Schillebeeckx has observed: 'The gospel is good news not just about Jesus but about the God of Jesus, the maker of heaven and earth, the God of all men and women .... We Christians learn to express stammeringly the content of what "God" is and the content of what "humanity" can be from the career of Jesus.' (*God Is New Each Moment*)

Perhaps the most, and the best, that can be said is: Jesus is the human person in whom God is fully present. But, even here, God remains Holy Mystery: divinity is shrouded in humanness.

Jesus Christ

The object of Christian faith is the person of Jesus Christ who briefly lived in the first century CE and now lives on in the Father's presence. The subject of our gospels is this Jesus Christ. The gospels, at once historical and theological, proclaim Jesus of Nazareth as the Christ, the definitive revelation of God. They make this proclamation in a language constructed of Christian theological and spiritual imagination aimed at eliciting a faith response. The proclamation embraces strictly historical elements (Jesus' death on the cross, for example) and theological interpretation in terms of biblical categories (for example, his ascent to God's right hand). The gospels present us with 'the earthly Jesus': a portrait of Jesus during his life on earth. This partial, theologically coloured picture has been examined and pored over by scholars of many disciplines, in a quest for 'the historical Jesus'. The historical Jesus is not the real Jesus but only a fragmentary reconstruction of him by modern means of research. But this reconstruction is of immense importance, particularly in our day. Jesus is an appealing and a challenging figure.

Gospel

Gospel is not a wholly distinctive literary form. It belongs to a broad Graeco-Roman genre of *bioi* – lives – or, more specifically, historical 'lives'. The purpose of a *bios* was, above all, to bring out clearly the nature of the subject. A gospel, as a life of Jesus (*bios Iesou*), highlights the uniqueness of Jesus as understood in theology. Our gospels are a mixture of narrative and discourse, centered on the person, life and teaching of Jesus of Nazareth, with special interest in his death and resurrection. All four evangelists were concerned to set out both the *story* of Jesus as well as what they took to be the *significance* of his activity and teaching, and their bearing on Christian life. He is the focus; he gives meaning to all.

A gospel is not objective biography; this story is shot through with resurrection faith. A gospel is written for believers: it is a Christian document addressed to Christians. More specifically, each gospel was, in the first place, written for a particular Christian community and with the needs of that community firmly in mind. The evangelists presented the 'facts' with the intention of bringing out the meaning that the events held for those who encountered them. They set out to voice the faith of the early church. The nucleus of that faith is that the crucified Jesus had been raised from the dead.

The fourth evangelist shows us the aim of an evangelist. The purpose of his selective presentation of the 'signs' of Jesus was in order that the Christian disciple might go on believing that the historical person, Jesus, is the Messiah of Jewish expectation, that he is the Son of God. He wrote so that, through their deepened faith in Jesus Christ, Christians might find life in him and live that life to the full (Jn 20:31). In other words, his concern was Christology and discipleship. The gospels are proclamations of the Good News. They are aimed at Christians striving to live the Christian Way.

The Gospel Jesus

We have looked at the object of Christian faith: the person of Jesus Christ who briefly lived in the first century CE and now lives on in the Father's presence. The gospels, at once historical and theological, proclaim Jesus of Nazareth as the Christ, the definitive revelation of God. Their proclamation of this Jesus is aimed at eliciting a faith response, and draws on the writers' theological understanding and their spiritual imagination, enriched by pondering on the Scriptures. The real or actual Jesus is the glorified Saviour in our midst. He will always be shrouded in mystery.

The total reality of any person is unknowable to human discernment – how much more the reality of the Risen One. The gospels present us with 'the earthly Jesus': a portrait of Jesus during his life on earth. This gospel picture is 'accurate', not in the sense that it is exact in detail, but that it is truth-bearing. It is the acceptance of this picture by the early believing community that guarantees the substantial truth of the gospel account. We will be looking at aspects of this gospel Jesus.

CHAPTER SEVEN

Jesus of Nazareth

Jesus of Nazareth was a Jew of the first century CE who began, lived and ended his short life in a minor province of the Roman Empire. Our information about him is meagre by historical standards. Apart from two brief statements, by the Jewish historian Flavius Josephus and the Roman historian Tacitus, our sources for knowledge of the historical Jesus are the canonical gospels alone. We really know nothing precise about the life of Jesus before the start of his mission. The infancy narratives of Matthew and Luke are primarily designed to demonstrate his place in fulfilling God's promises to the Chosen People and God's plans for the whole human race: in that way, they are christological texts. And they are not in total agreement. They tell us that Jesus was, quite likely, born in Bethlehem during the reign of Herod the Great. They all assert that Jesus was brought up in Nazareth of Galilee. Later, he was known as 'the Nazarene'. He was a *tekton*, an artisan (Mk 6:3) – not a well-paid technician of our day, but a village tradesman.

Nazareth

Nazareth was a small village, with a likely population of between 300 and 400, in southern Galilee, territory of Herod Antipas. It was an agricultural community of subsistence farmers. Joseph, Mary and Jesus belonged to this peasant world, in the lower artisan class. In Roman times, Galilean villagers were triply taxed: the traditional tithe for the support of the Jerusalem temple and priesthood; tribute to the Roman emperor; taxes to the local client-king, Antipas. This severe tax burden amounted to exploitation. Besides, there was the extra demand for the rebuilding of Sepphoris and the founding of Tiberias. Payment of taxes often involved borrowing that could lead to land being confiscated by creditors. Former farmers or tenant farmers could end up as day-labourers or beggars. This socioeconomic situation might have influenced the later conduct and preaching of Jesus.

The religious life of Nazareth was solidly Jewish. Jesus belonged to an observant household that lived out their faith in the one God of Israel in the rounds of ordinary daily life, in sabbath rest, and in prayer. Synagogue meant, most likely, more a village assembly than a building exclusively for religious purpose – the Greek word *synagoge* means an assembly or a congregation of people. The anchors of religious life were the family household and the public assembly, notably on the sabbath. There was also pilgrimage to Jerusalem. This must have been occasional because families under such severe economic stress could not readily take off on the three or so weeks needed for the journey. Later, Jesus, as itinerant preacher, would have wider scope.

Humanity

Our concern is the humanity of Jesus of Nazareth – the features that mark him firmly as one of us. The great Christian truth is that, in Jesus, God is really and truly present. His humanity is not the whole of it. The identity of Jesus is mystery in the strictest sense. To seek to define the mysterious reality of Jesus was and remains a formidable theological challenge. Today, in contrast to Christologies of the past, it is clear that we must wholly embrace his historical reality as a first-century Palestinian Jew. It is as such that he figures in our gospels. We instance a few traits of this authentic humanness.

Faith

The New Testament has a term for faith: *pistis*. It reflects its Old Testament background and means much more than 'belief' or intellectual assent. It means thoroughgoing commitment. It is the complete response, in total freedom, of a human to God in a spirit of trust, obedience, and endurance. Faith is letting God be God in one's life.

This was surely true of Jesus of Nazareth. He was, supremely, a man of faith. Increasingly, New Testament scholars acknowledge that, in Galatians and Romans, Paul understands *pistis Iesou Christou* (e.g. Gal 2:16, 20; 3:22; Rom 3:22, 26) as 'the faith *of* Jesus Christ' – his total trust in the Father and his own consequent faithfulness. Jesus lived his life in faith so understood: 'My food is to do the will of him who sent me and to complete his work' (Jn 4:34).

Jesus' faith, his total obedience to the Father, is well documented. Faith *and* hope – for hope is the other side of faith. This faith/hope is present in the 'after three days rise again' at the conclusion of each passion prediction (Mk 8:31; 9:31; 10:34). Before the raising of Lazarus he prayed: 'Father, I thank you for having heard me. I know that you always hear me' (Jn 11: 41-42). His prayer at Gethsemane – 'Not what I want, but what you want' (Mk 14: 35-36) – strikingly articulates his faithful obedience. At the Last Supper he spoke with assurance of drinking wine in the kingdom of God (Mk 14:62). He knew when his 'hour' had come and prayed to the Father to 'glorify' him so that the Father might be 'glorified', that is, revealed as the God of infinite mercy (Jn 17:1). A dying Jesus could confidently promise the 'good thief': 'Truly I tell you, today you will be with me in paradise' (Lk 23:43). And Luke gives, as the last word of Jesus, a prayer of utter serenity: 'Father, into your hands I commit my spirit' (23:46). He was, first and last, the faithful one, the faithful witness, *ho martys ho pistis* (Rev 1:5).

Love

'Which commandment is the first of all? (Mk 12:28). This question of a scribe to Jesus was one the rabbis sought to answer. They looked for a commandment that outweighed all the others, one that might be regarded as the basic principle on which the whole Law was grounded. Jesus had been asked to name a commandment; he responded by naming two commandments: 'You shall love the Lord your God with all your heart, and with all your soul, and with all your strength. The second is this, "You shall love your neighbour as yourself". There is no other commandment greater than these' (vv. 30-31). It would seem that Jesus was the first to bring together these two commands of love of God and of neighbour (see Deut 6:4; Lev 19:18). Love of neighbour arises out of love of God. He had taken and welded the two precepts into one.

In the synoptic gospels, only here and in the parallel passages (Mt 22:37 and Lk 11:42) is there word of human love of God. It appears sparingly in the rest of the New Testament. The emphasis is, rather, on God's love of humankind. And this is as it should be. It is because God has first loved us that we love God (Rom 5: 5, 8; 1 Jn 4:11). And there is the test of the authenticity of our love of God: 'Those who do not love a brother or sister whom they have seen, cannot love God whom they have not seen. The commandment we have from him [Jesus] is this: those who love God must love their brothers and sisters also' (1 Jn 4:20-21). Jesus had shown in his life and death the quality of this twofold love. His love for God motivated his total dedication to his mission. His love for humankind marked him as one who had come to serve the saving purpose of God, one who had laid down his life as a ransom for humankind (Mk 10:45; Jn 15:13).

Luke and John inform us of a quite special relationship between Jesus and the family of Martha, Mary and Lazarus in Bethany, and his friendship was warmest with the women. As a sexually mature man, he had an easy rapport with women, whom he treated with unfailing courtesy. On his final journey to Jerusalem 'Jesus entered a certain village' (Lk 10:38); from John 11:1 we learn that it was Bethany.

The warm relationship between Jesus and the women (Luke does not mention Lazarus), explicitly remarked in John 11:5 – 'Jesus loved Martha and her sister' – is, in Luke 10:38-42, graphically portrayed. An exasperated Martha does not hesitate to point out that it is Jesus' fault that she had been left on her own in preparation of a meal for Jesus and his disciples (v. 40). He gently chides her for her agitation (v. 41)

There is textual confusion with regard to v. 42a. The longer reading, impressively attested ('few things are necessary or only one'), refers to the needless concern of Martha – one dish will suffice. The shorter reading ('there is need of only one thing') may well be preferable: Martha is told that the one thing necessary is the presence of the Lord and the word that he imparts. He, indeed, is host rather than guest. Mary, drinking in his words (v. 39), is displaying 'undivided devotion to the Lord' (1 Cor 7:35). Here the role of Martha is contrasted with that of Mary: a disciple sitting at the feet of Jesus and listening to his word (Lk 10: 39a). A notable feature is the depiction of a woman as student of the word and the Lord's emphatic approval of the role.

Prayer

'Descended from David according to the flesh' (Rom 1:3). Jesus was a son of Israel. As an observant Jew he was, by definition, a man of prayer. Aside from Luke, who had a special interest in prayer, the evangelists do not elaborate on Jesus' prayer life. This is not surprising. Simply, they, like him, took prayer for granted. We, Christians of another culture and of the twenty-first century, cannot be so casual. We demand reasons for everything and we ask why we ought to pray in the first place. The realisation that Jesus was a man of prayer may give us food for thought. It is also a factor that underlines his humanity.

There is no doubt at all that Jesus did pray. Mark, with attractive candour, tells us that Jesus' addiction to prayer was something of a trial to his disciples. The evangelist has sketched a sample day in the early Galilean mission, at Capernaum (Mk 1:21-34), a day of enthusiastic reception and of great promise. His disciples, caught up in the excitement, were chagrined when Jesus went missing (v. 34) – 'In the morning, while it was still very dark, he got up and went out to a deserted place, and there he prayed' (1:35). Typically, Mark has said so much in few words. Jesus had slept (he 'got up'), had snatched a few hours of sleep. For his mission he needed deeper refreshment, a more potent source of energy, and he found it in prayer to his *Abba*. His Father was the Sustainer of all. As one 'like us in all things' (Heb 2:17), Jesus was wholly dependent on his God. He turned, spontaneously, to an *Abba* who would support him, who would back him in his endeavours. Though one sent, he had to plough his own furrow. But he was not alone because the Father was with him. The prayer of Jesus, his whole prayerful trust in his *Abba*, is an essential ingredient of any meaningful Christology.

Humour

It ought not surprise that Jesus had a refined sense of humour. This emerges notably in his parables The sower of Mark 4:3-7 had sowed haphazardly: on a busy pathway, on rocks, among thorns. Farmers would have scoffed at his stupidity. Jesus' hearers would have chuckled at the ludicrous picture of a man going about with a two-by-four sticking out of his eye as he peered to spot a speck in the eye of another (Mt 7:1-5). And there was that house-builder who sought a shortcut. The floor of a *wadi,* a dry riverbed, looked promising. Nice and level, and stones conveniently all about. He went ahead and built. The hearers would have laughed. What a nut! The winter floods would teach him a painful lesson (7:24-27).

In Luke 11:5-8 the suggestion of stubborn deafness to a friend's insistent request would have met with shocked disbelief: What boor would behave in such a disgusting manner? The gutsy widow (Lk 18:2-8) would have won a round of applause. Judges would not have been popular among a struggling peasant population – it was too well known that they favoured the rich. This widow had worn him down by sheer pestering. Good for her!

In Mark 7:24-30 the focus of the story is the dialogue between Jesus and the Gentile woman. She earnestly begged Jesus to heal her daughter. He refused because, as he told her, the rules did not permit it: 'It is not fair to take the children's food and throw it to the dogs' (v. 27). Jesus acknowledged the distinction between Jew and Gentile. The woman will not be put off by Jesus' refusal: all very well indeed – but even the dogs get crumbs! Jesus must have laughed. He had been trumped. This quick-witted woman had appealed to his sense of humour. He assured her that she need have no further worry: her sick daughter was well again.

Jesus' hearers must have appreciated the parable of the steward (Lk 16:1-8). They would have enjoyed the humour of his bold characterisation: his putting forward of a rascal as a spur to resolute decision and action. The manager (steward) had been accused of embezzlement. Until he produced his books he had a breathing space. He rewrote contracts in favour of his master's creditors and in hope of a kickback. It was a neat scam! The master, who had to honour the contracts duly made in his name, ruefully applauded the resourceful conduct of his unscrupulous manager. Jesus' outrageous story would have caught the attention of his hearers. His hope was that they would have caught his message: that his disciples show as much resourcefulness in God's business as men of the world do in their affairs.

Two other instances: The disciples were in a boat at evening, far out on a stormy lake (Mt 14:22-27). Suddenly, Jesus appeared, walking toward them on the waters of the lake. Peter, with bravado, offered to step out to meet him. Jesus bade him, 'Come'. Peter started out across the water, quickly panicked, and cried for help. Jesus must have smiled, with a shake of the head: typical Peter! And at Bethany, Jesus would certainly have smiled at Martha's scolding – 'Lord, do you not care that my sister has left me to do all the work by myself? Tell her then to help me' (Lk 10:40) – smiled because he knew his dear friend so well.

Prophet

Jesus was teacher and healer. But he was, pre-eminently, a prophet. In the Bible a prophet is God's spokesperson, one called and sent to proclaim the word of God. Old Testament prophets were very conscious of the call and of the task. We see this clearly when we look at an Amos, a Hosea, an Isaiah, a Jeremiah. 'The Lord took me from, following the flock ... and the Lord said to me, "Go, prophesy to my people Israel"' (Amos 7: 15); 'Then I heard the Lord, saying, "Whom shall I send? ... And I said, 'here I am, send me!' (Is 6:8); 'Before I formed you in the womb I knew you ... I appointed you a prophet to the nations' (Jer 1:5).

The call was a powerful summons; the task was challenging and formidable. There was need for commitment and courage. By and large, the prophetic word would not be heard. The task involved suffering and rejection – even death. Jeremiah is a poignant instance of the loneliness of the call: 'Under the weight of your hand I sat alone' (Jer 15:7). The mysterious prophetical figure of Second Isaiah paid the price in vicarious suffering: 'He was despised and rejected. He was wounded for our transgressions ... yet he bore the sins of many and made intercession for the transgressors' (Is 53:12).

Jesus of Nazareth was a prophet. As one who spoke – who was! – God's definitive word (see Heb 1:2), he was the eschatological prophet. As 'image of the invisible God' everything he did and said was manifestation of God. Jesus had served his prophetical apprenticeship under John the Baptist. His decision to launch his distinctive mission was based on a consciousness of a unique relationship with his *Abba*. He knew himself to be one called and sent: 'I must proclaim the good news of the kingdom of God ... for I was sent for this purpose' (Lk 4:43). The kingdom, the rule of God, is, in the long run, God himself as salvation of humankind. Salvation reaches into every aspect of human life. As with Elijah and Elisha, healing was part of Jesus' prophetic mission. This is explicit in his inaugural programme (Lk 4:14-30).

Coming to his Nazareth synagogue on a sabbath, Jesus was invited to take the Scripture reading. He opened the scroll of Isaiah and read out:

> The Spirit of the Lord is upon me,
> because he has anointed me to bring good news to the
> poor.
> He has sent me to proclaim release to the captives
> and recovery of sight to the blind,
> to let the oppressed go free,
> to proclaim the year of the Lord's favour (Lk 4:18-19).

He had taken care to close his reading before the next phrase of the Isaian passage – 'and the day of the vengeance of our God' (Is 61:2). 'Vengeance' would be no part of his message. Then he declared: 'Today this scripture has been fulfilled in your hearing' (Lk 4:21). This, then, is Jesus' programme as he embarks on his mission. His programme: good news to the poor ... freedom of captives ... relief of the oppressed. What is this but a form of liberation theology?

Religion

Like the Old Testament prophets, Jesus was a severe critic of religion. He was an observant Jew who wholly respected the authentic religious tradition of his people. He observed the sabbath; he was a regular attender at sabbath synagogue worship. He respected the traditional practices of almsgiving, prayer, and fasting (Mt 6:1-18). He went on pilgrimage to Jerusalem for the great feasts: Passover, Tabernacles, Dedication (Jn 2:13; 7:10,14; 10:22). He revered the temple as the house of God (Mk 11:17; Jn 2:16).

All the while, however, he was very critical of the manner in which, and the extent to which 'traditions' had overwhelmed religious practice. His own free attitude toward religion brought him into conflict with those for whom religion meant meticulous observance of rules and regulations. Jesus emerges both as an upholder and as a radical critic of religion. To be positively critical of any religious system is surely an attribute of maturity.

It is clear from the gospels that Jesus had authority (*exousia*) from God. It is equally clear that this power of his had no shade of domination. The gospels indeed show Jesus having facile authority over evil spirits (the exorcisms) and over nature (the stilling of the storm). But Jesus' authority did not extend to lording it over people. In relation to people he was largely helpless. The hallmark of his use of authority in relation to people was consistently and emphatically that of *diakonia*, service. If Jesus served others, it was always from a position of strength. He would not do what others wanted him to do unless it be consonant with God's will. He would lead, but he would not control.

Jesus certainly confronted the religious authorities, but without seeking to impose his authority on them. He was content to hold the mirror up to them, urging them to discern in their attitude and conduct a betrayal of God's rule. But that was the measure of it. Response was their responsibility. Jesus sought no advantage from his authority. He laid claim to no titles – it was up to others to identify him. He was, after all, the one who had come 'to serve, and to give his life as a ransom for many [all]' (Mk 10:45). In short, Jesus, in his authority, as in all else, mirrored God. For God, the God of infinite power, is never a God of force. The Son never would, nor ever did, resort to force.

In Mark 10:42-45 Jesus reads his ambitious disciples a sharp lesson. He solemnly asserts that, in the community of his disciples, there is no place for ambition. His church is a human

—

society; there is place for authority, for leaders. But those who lead will serve their brothers and sisters: the spirit of authority is service (*diakonia*). Surely Jesus had intended the paradox and had asked for it to be taken seriously. He first outlined the current standard of civil authority: domination, with leaders lording it over their subjects, making their presence felt in all areas of life (10:42). Then (v. 43) he asserted that this was not, positively not, to be the pattern for those who professed to follow him. Jesus stood authority on its head. Greatness would be measured by service: the leader will be slave (*doulos*) of the community. There could be no place at all for styles and trappings and exercise of authority after the model of civil powers and princes.

Is there anything in the Gospels quite as categorical as this demand. This word of Jesus was clear. Would it be heard? Not throughout Christian history. But it was heard in the Jerusalem of Jesus' day, and heard by the Roman power, heard as subversive of authority. Jesus was dangerous and had to be silenced. His teaching was political dynamite.

Sabbath

Sabbath observance is specified in well-nigh identical terms in both versions of the Ten Words or commandments: 'Remember the Sabbath day and keep it holy' (Ex 20:8; Deut 5:12). Apart from declaring it to be a day free of work, the *Torah* does not further specify how the sabbath is to be 'kept holy'. During the Babylonian Exile and especially in the subsequent Second Temple era an elaborate system of sabbath observance evolved. This formed a major feature of 'the tradition of the elders' which Jesus essentially rejected (see Mk 7:1-13).

Relevant here is the motive for sabbath observance proposed

—

in Deuteronomy. While in Exodus the sabbath is linked to God's sabbath rest (Ex 20:11), Deuteronomy links it to deliverance from Egyptian slavery: 'Remember that you were a slave in the land of Egypt, and the Lord your God brought you out from there with a mighty hand and an outstretched arm; therefore the Lord your God commanded you to keep the sabbath day' (Deut 5:15). In Jesus' view this celebration of freedom had, by his time, become a new slavery. It made no sense.

The frequent reference in the gospels to critique of Jesus' alleged violation of sabbath observance underlines his consistent attitude. He sought to set the sabbath free. That it needed to be set free is illustrated in the episode of Mark 3:1-6: an act of healing is regarded as a breach of sabbath observance. Note the querulous synagogue leader of Luke 13:1-14 in reaction to Jesus' healing of a crippled woman on the sabbath: 'There are six days in which work ought to be done; come on those days to be cured, and not on the sabbath day'. Jesus' assessment of sabbath observance is stated with emphatic clarity in the conflict story of Mark 2:23-28: 'The sabbath was made for humankind, and not humankind for the sabbath' (v. 27).

Indeed, the declaration is of wider import. Decoded, it reads: Religion is to serve men and women; men and women are not to be enslaved by religion. He had defined the true meaning of religion – it is *for* men and women.

Ritual observance

As the text of Mark 7: 1-23 stands, a precise incident lay behind Jesus' dispute with the Pharisees and scribes. They had observed that the disciples of Jesus did not practise the ritual washing of hands before meals. In their eyes this constituted a transgression of the 'tradition of the elders' – the *halakah,* or oral law.

Those Pharisaic traditions claimed to interpret and complete the Mosaic Law and were regarded as equally authoritative and binding as the Mosaic prescriptives. Later rabbis would claim that the 'ancestral law' constituted a second, oral, law given, with the written law, to Moses on Sinai.

In responding to the charge of neglecting one observance (Mk 7:5), Jesus turned the debate on to a wider issue: the relative worth of Mosaic law and oral law. He cited Isaiah 29:13 against the Pharisees, drawing a parallel between 'human precepts' of which Isaiah spoke and the 'human tradition' on which the Pharisees counted. Jesus rejected the oral law because it was the work of men (not the word of God) and because it could and did conflict with the law of God. The oral law had put casuistry above love. He instanced (vv. 9-13) a glaring example of casuistry run wild: a precise vow of dedication. A man might declare *korban* – that is, dedicated to God – the property or capital which, by right, should go to the support of his parents. Property thus made over by vow took on a sacral character; the parents had no more claim on it. In fact, such a vow was a legal fiction, a way of avoiding filial responsibility. But it was a vow and, as such, in rabbinical eyes, was binding and could not be dispensed. In this manner, a solemn duty enjoined by *Torah* (Ex 20-12), was set aside.

Jesus could multiply examples, he declared (Mk 7:13). He was aware that one whose mind runs to casuistry loses all sense of proportion. Minute detail becomes more and more important. Law and observance become an obsession. People are defined in terms of conformity or of 'sinful' departure from it. Casuists are regularly in positions of authority and make life miserable for others – especially the vulnerable. Jesus' concern was, first and always, *people* and their needs. Everything else was relative to that.

The criterion of clean and unclean (a strictly ritual principle) was at the root of Jewish concern with ritual purity. A saying of Jesus struck at the very distinction of clean and unclean, of sacred and secular: 'There is nothing outside a person that by going in can defile, but the things that come out are what defile' (Mk 7:15). At one stroke Jesus had set aside the whole concept of ritual impurity. Holiness does not lie in the realm of 'clean' over 'unclean.' It is not in the realm of things but in the realm of conduct. It is to be found in the human heart and is a matter of human responsibility. Mark's parenthetical comment – 'Thus he declared all foods clean' (v. 19) – correctly caught the nuance of the sayings.

More generally, it is a flat denial that any external thing or circumstance can separate one from God (see Romans 8:38-39). We can be separated from God only through our own attitude and behaviour. Jesus' contrast between word of God and human law, and his emphatic assertion of the priority of the former are, obviously, of abiding validity and moment. Religion has not always seen it so.

CHAPTER EIGHT

Champion of the Poor – Friend of Sinners

Champion of the Poor

Vocation

We have seen that the Old Testament bears witness to the God of Israel's preferential option for the poor and marginalised. We would expect to find this concern in the life and ministry of Jesus of Nazareth. And we do. Jesus knew it to be his vocation to proclaim the true God, the Father. He knew that, in faithfulness to his task, he was making the rule of God a present reality. How he saw his task is vividly portrayed in Luke's introduction to Jesus' ministry, Lk 4:18-19. Jesus pointed to the recipients of his good news: all who are weakest and powerless – 'the poor'.

The poor are not only those with few or no possessions. In the biblical context, the poor are the 'little people' who are incapable of standing up for themselves and hence, by reason of their need and sorry state, are God's cherished ones. The designation 'poor' (as in Luke's beatitudes, for instance) is not idealisation. The poor really do need help, the hungry stand in need of food, the mourning are visibly sorrowing. All cry out for compassion. Jesus knew these people. They are his people. The poor to whom he announced the good news and whom he pronounced blessed, are not those whom he proposed as models of virtue but are people literally 'down and out'. The kingdom of God, the consolation of the new age, is granted to the weak and despised – to those who suffer, and weep, and sorrow.

Wealth

Jesus' concern for the poor did not make him averse to the owning of property. But he was very clear that ownership involved social responsibility. In beginning his ministry, Jesus had abandoned his trade and was supported in his itinerant mission by relatively well-to-do women disciples (Lk 8:2-3). But Jesus did challenge wealth with severity where it had captured peoples' hearts and had blinded their eyes to God's purpose. Wealth induced a false sense of security (The Rich Fool, Lk 12:16-20), and blinded one to the plight of others (Dives and Lazarus, Lk 16:19-31).

The saying of Mark 10:25, 'it is easier for a camel to go through the eye of a needle than for someone who is rich to enter the kingdom of heaven', is a vivid example of the impossible (contrast of the largest beast known in Palestine with the smallest domestic aperture). The point is to underline in the strongest terms how hard it is for those who have wealth to divest themselves of their material possessions and the security and power that seem to come with them. The saying carries the further implication that salvation is ever God's achievement, never that of humans.

Compassion

Jesus displayed compassion throughout his mission. He consistently put people first. In Mark 6: 1-36 his attempt to find solitude for himself and his disciples was frustrated, but he was not annoyed. Instead, he was deeply touched by the earnestness of the crowd that had come to hear him, and by their need: 'He had compassion on them because they were like sheep without a shepherd' (v. 34). Further, at the second feeding (Mk 8:1-9), Jesus was moved to compassion by the people's physical need: 'I have compassion for the crowd, because they have been with me now for three days and they will faint on the way – and some of them have come from a great distance' (8:2-3).

Our gospels have two notably different versions of the beatitudes: Mt 5:3-12 and Lk 6:20-23. Matthew has nine beatitudes, Luke has four – but with four corresponding 'woes' (6:24-26). Both versions grow from an original that goes back to Jesus, the additions and adaptations being due to the evangelists. We can, without much trouble, discern a form of the beatitudes that would stand as a common basis for the development by the evangelists, and that may reasonably be regarded as the beatitudes of Jesus. These are three:

Blessed are the poor, for the kingdom is theirs.
Blessed are those who hunger, for they will be filled.
Blessed are the afflicted, for they will be comforted.

The beatitudes do not refer to three different categories but to three aspects of the same distressful situation. The first sets the tone. In declaring the poor blessed, Jesus gives concrete expression to the good news that he brings to the poor. The other two beatitudes make precise, and develop, the content of the first. The poor are the indigent, they are the hungry, they are those who lament their unhappy lot. These poor were coming to Jesus. Their present experience of poverty, hunger and tears played a decisive part in determining the object of their hope. Jesus was hope of the poor.

Women

We have looked at the 'poor' mainly in terms of the economically poor. But we have observed that the term can carry a wider brief to include the marginalized. In the world of Jesus' day, women fell into this category. In that culture the encounters of Jesus with women are remarkable. Not only are they frequent but, without exception, they are positive. This is clear in the wider setting of discipleship. Jesus began his mission by summoning disciples

The call of the first disciples (Mk 1:16-20) is a passage shaped to bring out the nature of Jesus' call and of the response – to show what 'following Jesus' means. The decisive factor is the person of Jesus himself. In order to become a disciple of Jesus it is not necessary to be an exceptional person. It was the impression of Jesus on Peter and his companions, reinforced by his personal word of call, that brought them into his following and made them his disciples. Mark was not intent on describing a scene from the ministry of Jesus. Rather, he was more concerned with the theological dimension of a typical call to discipleship.

In this context of discipleship the passage Mk 15:40-44 is of utmost significance. Mark says of the little group of women who witnessed the execution of Jesus: 'They used to follow him and provided for him when he was in Galilee; and there were many other women who had come up with him to Jerusalem' (v. 41). The women had 'followed him' – *akolouthein* is a technical term for discipleship. Although this is the only place in Mark where the discipleship of women is mentioned in explicit terms, we should not overlook the reference to 'many women'. We must recognise that in our gospels 'disciple' is an inclusive term. It is because they had continued to follow him if only 'at a distance' (v. 40) – as women they could not be at the very place of execution – that the final message is entrusted to these women (16:1-8). They alone, of all the disciples, had followed to the cross. Luke is the evangelist who gets the credit for alerting us to Jesus' solicitude for womankind. But Mark had, beforehand, made his telling contribution. These women disciples had stood steadfast and have not been ashamed of Jesus. They are those of whom the Son of Man will not be ashamed.

In John 20:11-18, John has reduced the 'women' of the synoptists to Mary Magdalene. Mary addressed a 'stranger'. She recognised him at his calling her by name. This is reminiscent of John 10:3 – the Good Shepherd 'calls his own sheep by name'. Her joyous instinct was to cling to him. She has to learn that her time for association with the earthly Jesus is past. His 'hour' was still in process – the 'hour' of death, resurrection and return to the Father. Mary was given a mission: apostle to the disciples. She carried a dramatic message. Up to now, in the narrative, Jesus alone was Son. Now he spoke of my Father and *your* Father, my God and *your* God! The God and Father of Jesus is God and Father of his 'brethren'. Christians are no longer Jesus' disciples, nor even his 'friends' (15:15) but his brothers and sisters This astounding truth was first confided to a woman.

This relationship of Jesus with women has repercussions. Salvation is salvation of *humankind*. Insistently, however, the place of women in the Church is seen as a problem that cannot be wished away. Jesus came to bring good news to the poor, to free the oppressed. It cannot be *his* will that his sisters remain second-class citizens in an institution that purports to be his Church. The patriarchal model does not square with his teaching and practice. Only an assembly of brothers *and* sisters can truly constitute his Church.

Children

If Jesus' attitude toward women was unconventional, no less so was his regard for children. The passage Mk 10:13-16 is a pronouncement story showing Jesus' attitude toward children. Mark has delightfully brought the little scene to life: mothers eager to present their little ones to Jesus; the disciples officiously 'protecting' Jesus and demanding, 'Get those brats out of here!'; Jesus' indignation at their rebuff to children; his taking them into his arms. The point of the narrative lies in the sayings. The disposition of a child – receptivity, a willingness to accept what is freely given – is necessary for all who would enter the kingdom. Children, better than any other, are suited for the kingdom. Since the kingdom, ultimately God as salvation of humankind, is a gift that must be welcomed with simplicity.

In Mark 9: 35-37 Jesus read a lesson to his disciples. He took a little child from the arms of its mother. 'Taking it in his arms' (v. 36) is proper to Mark (see 10:16), a vivid touch in his style. In that culture, no self-respecting man would have done the same. This little gesture spoke volumes of Jesus' reverence for people – especially the most helpless of all.

Friend of Sinners

In chapters 1 to 3 of the Letter to the Romans, the apostle Paul painted in stark colours the fate of humankind enslaved to Sin – *Hamartia* (sin personified). He did so as a foil to divine generosity: 'God proves his love for us in that while we still were sinners Christ died for us' (5:8). The offer of God's forgiveness was distinctive of Jesus' ministry. Indeed, he won notoriety as 'friend of sinners'. Traditionally, the challenge of Jesus has been modified in every conceivable manner. Here is a case in point. Jesus welcomed sinners – without condition. This was shockingly unconventional and a scandal to the righteous. Jesus was too much for the religious authorities of his day. He seems to be too much for the religious authorities of any day. Always, it seems, sinners can find the gap and encounter the gracious forgiveness and welcome of the God of Jesus – ever to the discomfiture of the righteous.

Scandal

The gospels make clear that Jesus' attitude towards sinners and his concern for outcasts was a scandal to the religious-minded. We may take it that those addressed in Matthew 21:31 ('Truly, I say to you, the tax collectors and the harlots go into the kingdom of God before you') are Jews who deny tax collectors and sinners the right to hope in God's forgiveness. The offence of the statement is its clear implication that the wretched prostitutes and detested tax collectors, scorned by the refined and the religious, are preferred by God to their despisers. Pharisees would be prepared to accept that God is merciful to sinners; they would not accept the unconditional forgiveness of God implicit in the role of Jesus.

In the earliest Jesus movement the Pharisees are not yet representative of a Judaism hostile to Christianity. They are Jews who perceived that Jesus was making an enormous and, to them, unacceptable claim. He was claiming that God takes the part of the poor and the outcast – simply because they are poor, deprived and despised. The rule of God was being inaugurated among the lowly and despised, not among the 'righteous'. This they could not and would not accept. At a further level, Jesus is rejecting any labelling or categorizing of people as 'sinners'.

The one distinctive note we can be certain marked Jesus' teaching about the rule of God is that it would include the 'sinners'. If we are truly to appreciate the scandal of the righteous at Jesus' befriending of sinners, we must understand who the sinners are. The term 'sinners' in the Old Testament refers to people who, in some fundamental manner, stand outside *Torah*, the Law. They are the 'wicked' *(reshaim)*. The Greek Old Testament rendered this term by *hamartoloi* ('sinners') and Greek-speaking Jews used the term to refer to the non-observant who, it was maintained, had thereby placed themselves outside the covenant. The 'sinners' of the gospels are these 'wicked' people regarded as living, blatantly, outside the Law. Jesus counted such within his fellowship. This was conduct that genuinely caused serious offence.

Table Fellowship

The story of Jesus feeding the multitude, attested in all four gospels, has association with a meal pattern throughout the ministry. Matthew (11:18-19) sets up a contrast between the Baptist and Jesus: 'John came neither eating nor drinking ... the Son of Man came eating and drinking, and they say, "Look, a glutton and as drunkard, a friend of tax collectors and sinners!"' The saying presupposes a well-established reputation. Jesus, unlike the Baptist, was no ascetic. This squares with Jesus' contention that, as long as he was with them, the disciples cannot fast (Mk 2:19).

Jesus showed his concern for the socially despised and for 'sinners' precisely through table fellowship with them. They had been stripped of hope by the 'righteous', who despised and avoided them. Now this manifest man of God went out of his way to break bread with them, to seek communion with them. He was assuring them that, unlike the righteous, God did not regard them as outcasts. Doubtless, he hoped that they would change their ways; but he did not threaten. And he did not demand that they perform what the Law stipulated if they were to be reckoned as righteous.

One thinks, for instance, of Zacchaeus in his sycamore tree. A preacher of repentance would have wagged the finger and read Zacchaeus – a spectacularly captive hearer – the riot act. Jesus casually invited himself to dinner in his home. Zacchaeus must nearly have toppled from his perch in surprised delight. A sermon would have left him unaffected – he had been too often preached at. The novel approach changed his life (Lk 19: 1-10). Jesus' concern reached out to all. He welcomed invitations to dine with Pharisees (see Lk 7:36; 14:1).

We may find the key to Jesus' understanding of his practice of table fellowship with outcasts in Matthew 8:11: 'I tell you, many will come from east and west and will eat with Abraham and Isaac and Jacob in the kingdom of heaven' (see Lk 13:28). His shared meals were a preparation for, and anticipation of, the great banquet in the kingdom. Hence, his pronouncement at the Last Supper: 'Truly I tell you, I will never again drink of the fruit of the vine until that day when I drink it new in the kingdom of God' (Mk 14:25). Moreover, in table fellowship with sinners Jesus was displaying the Father's preferential option for sinners (see Lk 15:7,10). If, then, at the Last Supper, Jesus asserted that his next drink of wine would be at table in the fullness of the kingdom, he implied that the supper was the climax of a series of meals that celebrated, in anticipation, the joy of the banquet. They were meals that, indeed, opened the banquet to all who would not deliberately reject the invitation.

Forgiveness

Jesus ben Sirach had regarded the forgiveness of our neighbour as crucially important for right human conduct (Sirach 28:2-4). We should expect nothing less from Jesus of Nazareth. His stance is manifest in Matthew 18: 21-35. Peter had come forward with a question: 'Lord, if another member of the church sins against me, how often should I forgive? As many as seven times?' (v. 21). He was, indeed, being generous and, obviously, expected Jesus' approval. To his chagrin, the answer came: 'Not seven times, but, I tell you, seventy times seven' (v. 22) – forgiveness without limit. The appended parable of the unforgiving servant (vv. 23-35) drives home the point, It also shifts the focus on to God's forgiveness of sin.

The disparity between the sums cited in the parable of Matthew 18:23-35 is gigantic – 10,000 talents is an unimaginable amount. A debt, impossible to repay, is written off casually by the king, and the debtor is not even fired. It is the situation one finds in Luke 15: 11-24. Yet one who had been shown such mercy cannot find it in his heart to remit a paltry debt. Not only that: he will not even give his fellow servant – his social equal – reasonable time and opportunity to repay. The king who had been moved with 'pity' (v. 27) is now 'angry' (v. 34).

The parable is a thinly veiled allegory. The 'king' is a merciful God who freely and lovingly forgives sin. Luke has painted the warmer picture of prodigal father and wayward son (Lk 15: 11-24). The reality is the same in either case. Like the younger son in the Lukan parable, this man, too, is forgiven with no strings attached. Faced with a cry of desperation, the forgiving God was moved with pity (Mt 15:27). But, when the recipient of such forgiveness cannot find it in his heart to be merciful, the master is angry (v. 33). Response to God's gracious forgiveness cannot be payment of a debt that is already fully remitted. It is, instead, warm thanksgiving for the blessing of such forgiving love. And the story in Matthew underlines the truth that sin, as God regards it, is man's inhumanity to man (even more sadly, man's inhumanity to woman), whatever shape that may take. Our abuse of others (and of ourselves) is an affront to the loving Parent who counts us as his children. Jesus clearly understood this because he knew his Father. A corollary: Jesus asks us, frail humans, to be forgiving without limit. He dares to ask the impossible because he knew that his God is the *Abba* whose forgiveness literally knows no limit.

Jesus and Sinners

The parables of Luke 15 that deal with the reprieve of sinners are Jesus' answer to the 'scandal' of the Pharisees: 'All the tax-collectors and sinners were coming to listen to him. And the Pharisees and scribes were grumbling and saying, "This fellow welcomes sinners and eats with them"' (15:1-2). When we add two sayings of Jesus, 'Those who are well have no need of a physician, but those who are sick; I have come to call not the righteous but sinners' (Mk 2:17); 'The Son of Man came to seek out and to save the lost' Lk 2: 17), and instance the generous response of a forgiven sinner (Lk 7:36-50), we get a thorough view of Jesus' regard for sinners.

The parables and sayings are a vindication of the good news for three reasons: because in them sinners are said to be sick people (only the sick need a doctor) and grateful people (only those burdened with debt know the relief of remission); because they reveal the nature of God as loving, merciful Parent; because they show sinners as, in some way, closer to God than the 'righteous'. Note the parable of The Pharisee and The Tax Collector (Lk 18:9-14).

These parables show God's compassion for sinners not as a timeless general truth but as realised in the ministry of Jesus. The lost sheep is dearer to the Shepherd, this Jesus, precisely because it is lost! The parables demonstrate that the words and deeds of Jesus are inseparable. He is not a teacher of morals outlining principles of conduct. Instead, his attitude toward the poor and daily life with them are the model of our behaviour. He has fulfilled perfectly – as he no doubt inspired – the words of counsel offered later to his disciples: 'Little children, let us love, not in word or speech, but in truth and in action' (1 Jn 3:18).

CHAPTER NINE

Death and Resurrection

Triumph of Failure

In some respects the painful Gethsemane episode (Mk 14: 32-42) is the most comforting in the gospels. There we see Jesus at his most vulnerably human. Hitherto, he had marched resolutely to meet his fate. Now that the dreadful moment is upon him, 'He began to be distressed and agitated' (v. 33). Jesus was shattered. It had been dawning on him what the Father seemed to be asking of him. He needed assurance that what God seemed to ask, he really did ask: 'Abba, Father, for you all things are possible, remove this cup from me; yet, not what I want but what you want' (Mk 14:36). Jesus explicitly prayed that the cup be taken from him. He did not contemplate suffering and death with stoic calm. He was appalled at the prospect. He knew fear. He was brave as he rose above his dread to embrace what the Father asked. But he must know if the path that opened before him was indeed the way his God would have him walk. He found assurance in prayer (14: 35, 36, 39).

His prayer did not go unanswered. As the Letter to the Hebrews puts it: 'He was heard because of his reverent submission' (Heb 5:7). That answer was: No! In traditional biblical imagery, Luke has dramatized the heavenly response: 'Then an angel from heaven appeared to him and gave him strength' (Lk 22: 53). Jesus was assured that it was indeed the Father's will that he tread the lonely road of total rejection. Not the Father's will as part of some cold, inflexible design. The Father was prepared to make a supreme sacrifice: 'Surely, they will respect my Son' (Mk 12:6). Jesus had understood that just here lay the victory over evil. For evil is finally helpless before a love that will never cry: Enough!

Reactions to Jesus

'This child is destined for the falling and the rising of many in Israel, and to be a sign that will be opposed' (Lk 2:34). The prophetic words of Simeon in Luke's infancy narrative really reflect later Christian knowledge of the historical mission of Jesus. Though he had come as the Saviour of his people (v. 11), he would be rejected by many of them (see Jn 1:11), for he would stand as a sign of contradiction, a stone that can be stumbling block or cornerstone depending on whether people turn their backs on him or accept him (see Lk 20:17-18; Acts 4:11; Rom 9:33; 1 Pet 2: 6-8). In his presence there can be no neutrality, for he is the light that people cannot ignore (see Jn 9:39; 12: 44-50), the light that reveals their inmost thoughts and forces them to take their part for him or against him.

Acceptance

'I was sent only to the lost sheep of the house of Israel' (Mt 15:2-4). Jesus' mission was to his own people. To them he proclaimed the kingdom of God, the rule of God, not alone in words but in his deeds of healing. The gospels assert that Jesus regularly attracted large crowds. It would appear that, on the whole, he met a favourable reception. It is not surprising that his healing ministry would have been warmly welcomed. Paradoxically, popular acclaim may have contributed to his death. The popularity was viewed by religious and political authorities as a threat. His teaching would not have been palatable to them. If he had spoken to deaf ears it might not have mattered. But he had a following. That was dangerous.

How deep ran the commitment of the 'crowds' we cannot say. Popular enthusiasm, as politicians know only too well, is fickle and ephemeral. Whether or not the ease with which the temple priests were able to turn the 'crowd' against Jesus is strictly historical, it is credible. Crowds had flocked to hear Jesus. There was no crowd to protest his crucifixion. Jesus was neither the first nor the last courageous prophetic figure to suffer a like fate. 'Like us in all things' indeed.

Disciples

There were those who 'followed' Jesus because they were called by him. These were 'disciples'. It is noteworthy that the word 'disciple' (*mathetes*), which occurs frequently in the gospels and Acts, is absent from the rest of the New Testament. It is associated with the mission of Jesus.

And it carries a specific meaning. Distinctive features of this initial discipleship were: Jesus took the initiative in calling; 'following' meant literal, physical following of an itinerant preacher; disciples were warned that they might face hostility and suffering. The evidence is clear that women, too, followed Jesus during his mission in Galilee and accompanied him on his last journey to Jerusalem (see Mk 15:40-41). This is wholly in keeping with Jesus' high regard for women.

From his disciples Jesus chose a core group – the Twelve (Mk 6:7). They symbolized the regathering, at the end of time, of all twelve tribes of Israel. The choice of the Twelve was a prophetic proclamation that God would re-establish his chosen people. After a single move to complete the number following the departure of Judas (Acts 1:15-26), it was quickly understood that the role of the Twelve was symbolic and pertained to the eschatological mission of Jesus himself. The Twelve, as such, had no role in the early church. Misleading deductions have been made from the fact that the Twelve were men. Indeed, Jesus had no choice. The Twelve symbolized Israel: twelve tribes descended from the twelve sons of Judah. They had to be men – the symbolism was fixed. What matters is that Jesus had chosen women, too, as his disciples.

There were also supporters of Jesus who had not been called to leave all and follow him. Some of them, men and women, are named in the gospels: Lazarus, Zacchaeus, Martha, and Mary. Surely there would have been others from among those who had been healed by Jesus. There was, then, within Israel, a solid core of those who would, after Easter, joyfully proclaim their faith in the risen Lord.

Opposition

Jesus was not welcomed by all. On the gospel evidence, he was constantly hassled by the Pharisees. Who were those Pharisees? They seem to have originated as a religious and political response to the programme of Hellenisation launched by Antiochus IV (175-163, BCE), ruler of the Seleucid kingdom that included Palestine, and his Jewish supporters.

The Pharisees perceived in this policy a threat to the very survival of the Jews as a distinct ethnic, cultural and religious entity. They emphasised detailed study and observance of the Law of Moses. They also possessed a normative body of tradition – the traditions of the 'fathers' or 'elders'. While they acknowledged that some of these legal rules and practices went beyond the Law, they maintained that such practices were nevertheless God's word for Israel. They actively engaged in striving to convince other Jews to observe these Pharisaic practices in their daily lives. Much of what is attributed to Pharisaic teaching refers to legal rulings or opinions regarding concrete behaviour (*halakoth*) in matters of purity rules, sabbath observance, marriage and divorce. After 70 CE and the destruction of the temple by the Romans, as practically the only religious group to have survived the Jewish War, their influence would have increased.

All four gospels attest to Jesus' frequent contact with Pharisees throughout his mission. Though they had much in common, their relationship was, not surprisingly, tense, because they both addressed the same constituency. They both sought to influence the main body of Palestinian Jews and win them to their respective visions of what God was calling Israel to be. Jesus would have challenged them directly and in parable. In prophetic mode, he may have pronounced 'woes' against them.

Yet, the gospels acknowledge that some Pharisees were willing to give Jesus a serious hearing (*e.g.*, Lk 7:36-50; Jn 3:1-2). Their relationship would have been notably less hostile than that represented in Matthew 23. As it stands, this text is an indictment of Pharisaic Judaism painfully reflecting the bitter estrangement of church and synagogue toward the close of the first century CE. It is significant that Pharisees are practically absent from all passion narratives. The death of Jesus was brought about, historically, not by Pharisees, but by an alliance of the Jerusalem priesthood and Roman political authority.

Rejection

Priests were most active in the passion narratives. Indeed, the gospels give the impression that the priestly aristocracy was principally involved in bringing Jesus to his death. The temple priests would have had little interest in a Galilean layman until

---

they began to look upon him as a threat. Jesus' critique of the temple emerged as an accusation at his trial. His prophetic gesture in 'cleansing' the temple (Mk 11:15-17) was very well understood: 'When the chief priests and the scribes heard it, they kept looking for a way to kill him' (v. 18). Luke tells us (Acts 7) that his critique of the temple sealed Stephen's fate. It is hazardous to challenge entrenched religion. There was also the charge of 'blasphemy' (Mk 14:64). However the high priest understood the term, he was branding Jesus as a heretic and deserving of death. He was, besides, a messianic pretender (vv. 61-62).

There was the threatening spectre of a messianic uprising and consequent trouble with Rome. The Fourth Gospel voices the fear: 'This man is performing many signs. If we let him go on like this, everyone will believe in him, and the Romans will come and destroy both our holy place and our nation' (11:47-48). The high priest Caiaphas gives voice to cynical political expediency: 'You know nothing at all! You do not understand that it is better for you to have one man die for the people than to have the whole nation destroyed' (vv. 49-50). This heretic and politically dangerous man had to go – an all-too-human situation.

The snag was that the Sanhedrin could not carry out a death sentence. The Romans had to be involved (see Jn 18:31). The messianic title 'King of the Jews', which runs through all four passion narratives, served their purpose: it could be given blatant political emphasis. In Pilate's eyes, a claim to be king independently of Roman approval was high treason. The temple priests won Roman sanction and the fate of Jesus was sealed.

And they crucified him

There is a strange poignancy about the death of Jesus, a tragic quality that is caught superbly by Mark. Jesus' death was brought about by human connivance. Jesus was at once a religious and a political hazard. His preaching of good news to the poor was a threat to the establishment, a threat to the religious authorities and to the state. That voice had to be silenced. Together they condemned him to death.

As he moved toward the cross, Jesus was left more and more alone: betrayed by one disciple, denied by another, abandoned by all. Even his fellow sufferers disowned him. Most terrible of all, he suffered the absence of God: 'My God, my God, why have you forsaken me?' (15:34). He now knows what it costs to give his life as a ransom for all (10:45).

The grim drama was being played out. Crucified at the third hour (9 a.m.), Jesus had spent three hours in agony. Now, at the sixth hour (noon) the hour of darkness and of momentary demonic triumph broke in – 'your hour, and the power of darkness' (Lk 2:53; see Amos 8:9-10). Jesus had begun his mission in an encounter with Satan (Mk 1:12-13), and carried on the war in his exorcisms. Now, helpless on the cross, he seemed to be crushed by these very powers. The close of that time of darkness (symbolic theological darkness), the ninth hour (3 p.m.), marked the hour of fulfilment.

Paradoxically, it seemed to sound the nadir of Jesus' defeat. This is brought out by the twofold reference to a 'loud cry' – *phone megale* in Greek. Mark uses this expression four times: twice to describe the loud cry of the demoniac (1:26 and 5:7) and twice referring to the reaction of Jesus himself to the intolerable pressure of evil (15:34, 37). He suffered the absence of God. His cry of dereliction was one of total desolation: 'My God, my God, why have you forsaken me?' His words are the opening of Psalm 22, a lament. A lament is the cry of a suffering righteous person addressed to the One who can bring an end to suffering. Mark has Jesus die in total isolation, without any relieving feature at all. It would have seemed that, up to this point, Jesus' isolation could go no further: deserted by his disciples, taunted by his enemies, derided by those who hanged with him, suffocating in the darkness of evil. But the worst was now. His suffering was radically lonely. But his God was *my* God (v. 34). Even in this, as at Gethsemane, it was 'not what I want, but what you want'.

Here, even more than earlier, the sheer humanness of Jesus was manifest. And his experience was a thoroughly human one. It underlines the difference between feeling and reality. The feeling: one of God-forsakenness. The reality: never were Father and Son more at one. It is akin to the experience of Job, who also suffered the absence of God, or of later mystics suffering the 'dark night of the soul'. God had never withdrawn; the feeling was that he had.

Jesus had cried out, *Eli*, 'my God'; the bystanders thought he had called on Elijah, who was popularly believed to come to the aid of the just in tribulation. Misunderstanding hounded Jesus to the end. 'Sour wine' is the Roman soldiers' *posca* - a cheap red wine. The gesture was kindly meant (v. 36), but Mark, likely with Psalm 69:21 in mind ('They gave me gall for my food, and for my thirst they gave me vinegar to drink') thinks of it as an addition to Jesus' misery. Once again the 'loud cry' is significant: it depicts his consciousness of his struggle with evil. All the more so because v. 37 describes a sudden, violent death; 'breathed his last' is not strong enough to carry Mark's meaning. Jesus died abandoned, seemingly crushed by the forces of evil. This is perfectly in keeping with Mark's *theologia crucis*. Forthwith, he will be able to point to the victory of Jesus.

At the end of the passage, verses 27-29, Mark focuses on the theme of Jesus as 'the Son of God'. An emphatically positive

response to Jesus' death contrasts with the mocking challenges hurled at the dying Jesus (15:29-32), when the Roman
centurion in charge declares in awe: 'Truly, this man was God's
Son!' (v. 39).

Note that the temple curtain had just been rent from top
to bottom (v. 38): the temple had lost its significance (see 11:
12-25; 13:2; 14:54) as centre of the cult through which God,
had mediated forgiveness of sin and salvation. The temple
curtain 'was torn' – by God! Jesus, who had suffered the pangs
of Godforsakenness, was now vindicated. Salvation is henceforth mediated through the shedding of the blood of the Son
of God. It is as Jesus had proclaimed to his disciples, 'the Son
of Man came not to be served but to serve, and to give his life
as a ransom for many [all]' (14:24). The temple is gone. God's
Son is now the locus of salvation. While the chief priests had
demanded that 'the Messiah, the King of Israel, come down
from the cross now, so that we may see and believe' (v. 32), it
was a Gentile who saw and believed. The Roman centurion's is
a profession of Christian faith. It confirms Mark's theological
position. The revelation of God's Son took place on the cross.
It was triumph of failure.

Failure?

The truth is that his death marked Jesus as a failure. Jesus was
executed on the order of a Roman provincial official. An alleged troublemaker in that bothersome province of Judea had
been dealt with. The incident did not cause a ripple in impe-
rial affairs. Yet history has shown that this execution was an
event of historic proportions. Its ripples flow strongly 2,000
years later. Let us be clear. The Romans and Jewish Sanhedrin
had effectively closed the 'Jesus case'. The message and aims

of Jesus, and his life itself, had ended in ignominious death. His prophetic voice had been muzzled. This is failure.

The question is: Why had Jesus been silenced? It was because he had lived and preached, unflinchingly, God's love for humankind. That is why he had table fellowship with sinners, why he sought to free women and men from the tyranny of religion, why, at every turn, he bore witness to the true God. In face of the threatening opposition, he might have packed it in and gone home to Nazareth. That would have been failure indeed. They might take his life, but to his last breath he would witness. What Jesus tells us is that failure is not the last word – that is, as God views failure.

From God's point of view, there could be no question of failure in the fate of Jesus. This is what John brings out dramatically in his gospel. He undoubtedly knew the tradition behind the synoptic gospels but he chose to turn their tragedy into triumph. What is important for us in his presentation is that he stressed what the others imply: failure is not the last word. But what Mark has done is of equal importance. He has shown that a sense of failure, even for Jesus, is a grievous human experience.

There is a further point. Too often the resurrection of Jesus is presented as a rescue operation. As someone has put it graphically, it is like the climax of a Western movie when the beleaguered wagon train is saved by a troop of U.S. cavalry appearing out of the sunset. The truth is that resurrection is inherent in the life and death of Jesus. His 'failure' was his total commitment to God and to humankind. That historical moment of failure on the cross was God's overcoming of human failure. If Paul can declare of the Christian that nothing in all creation can separate him or her from the love of God (Rom 8:39), then a death motivated only by love cannot, for a moment, cut off Jesus from his God. The human cry of God-forsakenness is heavy with feeling. The reality is quite other: never were Son and Father more wholly one. The ultimate helplessness of death was disclosed: 'God raised him up, having loosed the pangs of death, because it was not possible for him to be held by it' (Acts 2:24).

To the End

'Jesus ... having loved his own who were in the world, he loved them to the end' (Jn 13:1). 'To the end' (*eis telos*) means more than steadfastness to the last. The phrase can be adequately rendered in some such fashion as: he showed them how utterly he loved them. Jesus would show his 'greater love' (Jn 15:13) by dying for the principles he steadfastly believed in, principles he so earnestly wanted his disciples to embrace. He knew that his death would awaken them to the seriousness of his demands and would inspire them to be faithful to his ideals. They, in turn, would display to the world the true visage of the Father.

Jesus laid down his life in loving response to the Father's love. The Father did not demand the death of Jesus. The Father gave his Son for humankind, and gave him *eis telos*. He would show human beings that his love for them was in deadly earnest. The Father did not bring about the death of his Son; Jesus died at the hands of his religious and political enemies. But the Father did not shrink from having him 'delivered up' to his enemies. Only so does the death of Jesus fall within 'the definite plan and foreknowledge of God' (Acts 2:23). And, in filial acceptance of God's saving purpose, and only so, did Jesus accept death.

We should be clear, however, that the 'definite plan' of God does not envisage an inflexible divine strategy. It is, in fact, a manner of saying: *We* do not know why the Son, the sinless one, had to suffer and die, *God* knows. Jesus laid down his life in loving response to the Father's love – love of the Son and of humankind. He was obedient unto death, with an obedience that was a loving 'Yes' to a purpose of sheerest love. 'God so loved the world...' There is no gainsaying that word. It is the only explanation of the death of Jesus that is consonant with the character of our God.

A Mistaken View

The eleventh-century theologian Anselm, later archbishop of Canterbury, wrote a celebrated thesis (*Cur Deus Homo*) in response to the question: Why was it necessary for Jesus Christ to die in order for God to forgive human sin? His answer, later known as the satisfaction theory, became dominant over the centuries and is still in vogue today. Unhappily, it is a wholly mistaken view. Because this is so and because many are still influenced by it, it is needful to treat of it here.

Anselm's cultural context was the world of feudalism. A central value in the feudal world was the honour of a feudal lord. If a feudal lord were dishonoured, there were two responses: punishment or appropriate reparation. God was imaged as a feudal Lord. When humans sin, they offend God. God's dignity is infinite. The satisfaction sinners owe is also infinite. And who can pay that? The answer is: Jesus Christ. Being human, Christ makes amends in the name of sinful humanity. Being divine, the reparation is of infinite scope. At first sight, the perfect answer. In reality, the theory is fatally flawed.

In the first place, God is *not* a feudal lord. And, from the beginning, long before the death of Jesus, God is merciful and forgiving. Next, the death of Jesus is presented as *neces-*

sary for salvation. This shows a God ungraciously forgiving sin, provided he gets his pound of flesh – ultimately seeming to demand human sacrifice! It is a disastrous image of God. Besides, the death of Jesus is taken in isolation – there is no reference, in this theory, to the resurrection. But the resurrection is God's approval of the death of Jesus, not as satisfaction for sin, but as the ultimate expression of the forgiving, saving, love of Father and Son. Simply put, God did not demand the death of his Son, did not need the death of his Son. Instead, 'God so loved the world that he gave his only Son' (Jn 3:16). It is over time to abandon the satisfaction theory.

Resurrection

When, in 1 Corinthians 15, Paul energetically defends the reality of resurrection from the dead, he starts by appealing to the resurrection of Jesus (15:3-8). It is clear from the New Testament that Christians were, from the outset, convinced that the crucified Christ was not held by death. In Jewish faith and prayer, God is he who 'makes the dead live'. Jewish faith and hope looked to a resurrection of the righteous at the end of time.

The first Christians asserted that, in the person of Jesus of Nazareth, this divine act had taken place. Jewish expectation was eschatological: resurrection was an event of the end-time. Christians were asserting that an eschatological event had taken place in time. If one may put it so, the resurrection of Jesus is an event at once eschatological and historical. In essence, it is a spiritual event beyond our world of time, and yet it has impinged on our world of time. Paul uses the word *ophthe* to state that Christ appeared to Cephas, to the other witnesses listed, and to himself. The term can be rendered 'he showed himself'. It means that the risen Jesus manifested himself as present in some fashion so that Paul, and the others, can say, 'I have seen the Lord'. A divine initiative leads to real experience of the presence of the Lord and a firm conviction of the reality of this presence. Something had happened to these men and women that they could only describe by saying that they had 'seen the Lord,' that the Lord had 'shown himself' to them. The phrase did not refer to some general Christian experience, but rather to a particular series of occurrences confined to a limited period.

Such occurrences, on the threshold of ordinary human experience, would simply not submit to precision of detail. Only symbol and imagery, not literal prose, could tell *this* story. The evangelists can write of the death of Jesus – death we recognise. But there is no attempt to relate the wholly mysterious fact of his being raised from the dead.

It is evident from our Gospels that the resurrection of Jesus is not at all the resuscitation of a corpse in the sense of a return to earthly life. The resurrection of Jesus means his rising to life beyond death. The risen Jesus lives a life that transcends earthly life; he has broken out of the confines of time and place. The risen Jesus was present to his disciples in a new and unfettered manner, and not only to his original disciples. He is present, potentially, to all men and women through time and history.

This abiding presence is implied in Matthew 28:20: 'I am with you always, to the end of the age'. He is the same Jesus of his earthly life, but now transformed. Paul can declare: 'The last Adam [Christ] became a life-giving Spirit' (1 Cor 15:45), living a Spirit-life now and no longer a life of flesh. Christians came to understand that 'eternal life' is life with God and with the risen Jesus. That conviction is enshrined in the promise to the 'good thief': 'Truly I tell you, today you will be with me in paradise' (Lk 23:43). Instead of trying to situate or describe 'paradise', it is more profitable to recall the comment of Ambrose: 'Life means living with Christ. Where Christ is, there too is life, and there is the kingdom' (*Vita est enim esse cum Christo: ideo ubi Christus, ibi vita, ibi regnum*).

CHAPTER TEN

God Is Love

No one has ever seen God; the only Son, who is close to the Father's heart, he has made him known (Jn 1:18).

The God who did not will to be alone created humankind. Loving Parent, he constantly called out: 'Here am I, here am I' (Is 65:1). He waited for a response, waited not only in patience but with divine compassion. And, from that human race, in God's good time, issued the one who responded, wholly. In him, the perfect response to God, God could be, God would be, God in history. God could, God now would, enter wholly into human joy and human sorrow. God would have, to the full, compassion with women and men in their pain and in their death. It was his purpose from the start. 'God remembered Noah' (Gen 8:1): he would henceforth bear with humankind. 'The Lord said to Abram' (12:1): he launched his plan to save humankind. 'He did not spare his own Son' (Rom 8:32): God showed that he really is God *for us*.

Who, then, is God? Our God is Father of our Lord Jesus Christ who has shown himself in the life and cross of Jesus. God is truly the God of the Old Testament whom Jesus addressed as *Abba*. The difference is that, through revelation by the Son, we see God more clearly. The New Testament brings more sharply and emphatically before us a concerned and caring Parent: 'God so loved the world that he gave his only Son' (Jn 3:16). God is the Father who has given us the Son – given us himself. We measure love by our experience of love. When we strive to measure divine love we need to think the unthinkable, believe the unbelievable. God has revealed himself to us in the human person, in the life, death and resurrection of Jesus of Nazareth. In him, God has come to walk with us. In him God has suffered among us and at our hands. It is always the same God, the one God, from the first page of the Bible to the last. Our image of God, how we perceive God, is crucial. The simple, but profound, truth: God is Love.

The Cross, God's Foolishness

For Jews demand signs and Greeks desire wisdom, but we proclaim Christ crucified. A stumbling-block to Jews and foolishness to Gentiles, but to those who are called, both Jews and Greeks, Christ the power of God and the wisdom of God. For God's foolishness is wiser than human wisdom, and God's weakness is stronger than human strength (1 Cor 1:22-25).

Theology of the Cross

In face of folly-and-scandal Paul would proclaim the Cross – because the Cross showed forth, with stark clarity, the saving will and saving power of God. One may ask: Why should the death of Jesus have power to save? How does this saving come to pass? Paul saw that the answer must lie with God: 'God was in Christ, reconciling the world to himself' (2 Cor 5:19) – there is the answer. God is active in the Cross. Reconciliation of sinful humankind is God's deed, not ours: 'God reconciled us to himself through Christ' (v.18). Salvation, attainment of true humanness, is, in the last resort, God's achievement. For the answer to the primal temptation to be like God (Gen 3:5), is to let God be God in one's life. That is the lesson of the Cross.

The wisdom of the 'foolish' God was demonstrated on the Cross. Where is God? The God absent to human eyes was most present at Calvary. A God of paradox, surprising us, a God displaying God's power. The wisdom is the saving will and saving power of God. The saving power is reconciliation. The Cross shows a helpless Jesus wholly turned to God – humanness wholly open to God. The Cross shows Jesus as, radically, Son of God and humans as children of God. The Cross shows the earnestness of a gracious God, shows that there is no limit to his desire to win humankind to himself. He is a God 'who did not withhold his own Son, but gave him up for all of us' (Rom 8:32). In the Cross he has put in his claim – his call for our surrender to his parental love.

God reconciles us sinners to himself through Christ – specifically through his death. Historically, the death of Jesus was an unjust and brutal execution. Jewish religious and Roman political authorities connived at getting rid of a 'troublemaker'. The mercy of God is not dependent on the death of Jesus. Divine mercy does not require the torture and violence of crucifixion. In the passion of the Son, God took upon God's own self all the suffering of the world and, by absorbing it, put it out of commission. Evil can ultimately be overcome only by love: 'For God so loved the world that he gave his only Son' (Jn 3:16).

In the Cross God shows what it is to be human. God's Son dramatically demonstrates the radical powerlessness of the human being. he shows that we are truly human when we accept our humanness, when we face up to the fact that we are not masters of our fate. As Jesus was stripped of his clothes so, too, he displayed a humanness stripped of every illusion. And nowhere more than there did he manifest himself as the one come to serve. On the cross Jesus manifested himself as the one who had yielded himself wholly to his God. The Cross offers the authentic definition of humanness: God's definition. There he starkly, firmly, reminds us of what we are. On the Cross God defines the human being as creature – not to crush or humiliate but that he may be, as Creator, wholly with his creature. On its own, humankind has indeed reason to fear. With God, in total dependence on God, there is no place for fear.

Humankind stands in need of redemption. Paul was very clear on that score. God took the initiative. He laid claim on us and has given us a claim on him. He is God for us – the loving God who created us and calls us to be his daughters and his sons. The giving of the Son shows, beyond doubt, that God is in deadly earnest. God is ever the Father of the 'prodigal son' who looks eagerly for the homecoming of the child (the sinner), who is ready to take off and embrace him fondly when he appears on the horizon.

Salvation

When it comes to salvation, Paul knows no distinction (Rom 3:22): faith in Jesus Christ is now and henceforth the only path to salvation for Jew and Gentile alike. All humankind had 'fallen short of the glory of God' (3:23), that is to say, was no longer truly in the image of God. The root of our failure is the human propensity to put non-gods in the place of God. When we acknowledge God's claim on us the image is restored.

Because he lays claim to us as sinners we are justified 'as a gift' (3:24). By letting God be 'just', by letting him be gracious in our regard, we are renewed, we are re-created. God's saving power – that is what 'grace' means – brings about the new creation. By relying solely on Christ, God's saving presence among us, we are set free from our attempts to make ourselves acceptable by creating congenial gods. For Paul, it is Christ who reveals the power of God, particularly in his death. In him the saving lordship of God has put in an appearance and is really here.

The Faithful Friend

> While we were yet sinners, at the right time, Christ died for the ungodly ... God shows his love for us in that while we were yet sinners Christ died for us (Rom 5:6,8).

It is the clearest possible proof that God loves humankind, sinful as we are. 'The ungodly': Jesus died for those who were estranged from God. Paul stresses the love revealed in the fact that God, in Jesus, went to such lengths on our behalf.

> If while we were yet sinners we were reconciled to God by the death of his Son, much more, now that we are reconciled, shall we be saved by his life. Not only so, but we also rejoice in God through our Lord Jesus Christ, through whom we have now received our reconciliation (5:10-11).

We have received our reconciliation because on the Cross the human person is truly human, nothing other than God's creature. By saying yes to God's deed in Jesus – faith – we acknowledge that reality. Reconciliation: God wants us to be his friends. To be set right with God is to have him as a faithful friend.

Children of God

> All who are led by the Spirit of God are children of God ... When we cry 'Abba! Father!' it is the Spirit himself bearing witness with our spirit that we are children of

God, and if children then heirs, heirs of God and fellow heirs with Christ, provided we suffer with him in order that we may also be glorified with him (8: 14-17).

The Spirit – God's loving presence in our world – has brought about a second transformation, the transformation of 'slave' into 'child'. God's Spirit makes us members of God's family. It lets us address God as Jesus did: *Abba*. If we share God as Father with Jesus, then we are children of God and members of God's family. That is our human destiny – but we had lost sight of it. The Spirit must bring the Christian to an awareness of this remarkable situation.

The God who has adopted us as his children awakens in us an awareness of that fact and then helps us in our wondering acknowledgment of that fact: *Abba*! 'Provided we suffer with him': suffering at the hands of a world dominated by 'flesh' (Paul's term for sinful humanity) is a sign that we no longer belong to that world. Suffering – 'if we share in the Cross': Paul will not hear of a 'Christianity' which claims to have found union with the risen Christ and yet seeks to avoid the Cross in life *now*.

The Love of God

What then are we to say about these things? If God is for us, who is against us? He who did not withhold his own Son, but gave him up for all of us, will he not with him also give us everything else? Who will bring any charge against God's elect? God who justifies! Who is to condemn? Christ Jesus, who died, yes, who was raised, who is at the right hand of God, who indeed intercedes for us! Who will separate us from the love of Christ? Will hardship, or distress, or persecution, or peril, or the sword?

... No, in all these things we are more than conquerors through him who loved us. For I am convinced that neither death, nor life, nor angels, nor rulers, nor things present, nor things to come, nor powers, nor height, nor depth, nor anything else in all creation, will be able to separate us from the love of God in Christ Jesus our Lord (Rom 8:31-39).

This great peroration celebrates the victory of God's love. It is vulnerable love: God 'did not withhold his own Son' (8:32). Having committed himself wholly, he will not tolerate any hitch to his saving purpose. Trials and sufferings of this age will not frustrate love of Father and Son for us (8:35-36). 'We are more than conquerors through him who loved us' (8:37). This love of Christ was concretely shown in his giving himself up to death on our behalf. Paul himself lived his Christian life 'by the faith of the Son of God who loved me and gave himself for me' (Gal 2:20). He was happy to put his trust wholly in the faithfulness of Christ.

This remarkable declaration of Paul's certainty of salvation is a summary of the whole first part of Romans – and, it might be said, of Paul's Gospel in general. It tells us that God's love is like this. It assures us that here is the God who has laid claim to us and given us a claim on him. We learn at once who God is: he is God for us. It is as good a definition of God as we might hope for. God is the loving God who created us and called us to be his daughters and his sons. The question of verse 32 – 'He who did not withhold his own Son, but gave him up for all of us, will he not with him give us everything else?' – can have one answer only. The giving of his Son shows, beyond doubt, that God is in deadly earnest. Father and Son were prepared to go to any length to save humankind from itself. God gave his Son without any precondition: God took the risk. The death of the Son was, at the deepest level, a sacrifice made by God.

Here, Mark 12:1-12 is illuminating. The parable of The Wicked Vinedressers is specifically designed to bring out the theological significance of the death of Jesus. It is allegory. The vineyard is Israel; the tenants become, at the end, the chief priests and scribes and elders. The rejected and maltreated servants are the prophets. The climax is the sending of the son. It is the master's final card: 'They will respect my son'. The last thing the master desired was the death of his son. The message is unmistakable. God did not desire the death of his Son; he did not need the death of his Son. He took a colossal risk: 'God did not spare his own Son'.

There is a division of opinion as to how verses 33-34 of the text from Romans should be punctuated. The preferred choice here is of two questions with ironical answers. Who can bring a charge? God – who justifies! It is really another way of putting the question of v. 31 – 'If God is for us, who is against us?' Can we imagine that the God who, in our helplessness, has, at such a cost, taken his saving initiative is now going to be our Judge? And who will condemn us? Christ Jesus who died for us, who intercedes for us! Again it is another way of putting a question: 'Who will separate us from the love of Christ?' Christ's love for us is dramatically manifest in his sacrificial death and in his efficacious intercession. Tribulations and distress cannot separate us from the love of Christ. It is evident that the suffering in question is especially suffering that comes in the service of the Gospel. It follows, though, that no trials of our human lot can come between the Christian and that unyielding love.

With the Jewish and Hellenistic worlds of his day in mind, Paul insists, for those who believed that angelic beings had influence over humans, and for others who believed in astrology, that none of these 'forces' had any effect on God's love for us. The simple fact is that nothing in the whole of creation – which is God's creation – can come between us and God's love for us, concretely expressed in the unqualified giving of his Son for our sake. It has been finely said: 'There is no arguing with such a certainty. Either you simply don't believe it or you recognise it as the word of God'.

Further Reading

Bruce C. Birch, *et al. A Theological Introduction to the Old Testament* (Nashville: Abingdon Press, 1999).

Walter Brueggemann, *Theology of the Old Testament* (Minneapolis: Fortress, 1997).

James D. G. Dunn, *Christianity in the Making. Vol. 1. Jesus Remembered* (Grand Rapids, MI: Eerdmans, 1998).

John C. Dwyer, *Son of Man and Son of God* (New York: Paulist Press, 1983).

Elizabeth Schussler Fiorenza, *In Memory of Her. A Feminist Theological Reconstructuring of Christian Origins* (New York: Crossword, 1983).

Pope Francis, *Laudato Si'. On Care for Our Common Home* (Libreria Editrice Vaticana, 2015).

Terence E. Fretheim, *The Suffering God* (Philadelphia: Fortress, 1984).

Abraham Heschel, *The Prophets*. Vol. II. (New York: Harper & Roe, 1962).

Elizabeth A, Johnson, *Quest for the Living God* (New York/London: Continuum, 2007).

— *Ask The Beasts: Darwin and the God of Love* (London: Bloomsbury, 2004).

— *Creation and the Cross. The Mercy of God for a Planet in Peril* (New York: Maryknoll, 2018).

Herbert McCabe, O.P., *Faith Within Reason* (London: Continuum, 2007).

John P. Meier, *A Marginal Jew, Vol I: Rethinking the Historical Jesus. Vol. II: Mentor, Message and Miracles* (New York: Doubleday, 1991, 1994).

Francis J. Moloney, The *Gospel of John*. Sacra Pagina 4. (Collegeville MN: Liturgical Press, 1998).

— *The Gospel of Mark: A Commentary.* (Peabody, MA: Hendrickson, 2002).

Jurgen Moltmannm, *The Crucified God* (London: SCM, 1974).

Albert Nolan, O.P., *God in South Africa. The Challenge of the Gospel* (Grand Rapids: Eerdmans, 1988.

— *Jesus Today: A Spirituality of Radical Freedom* (Maryknoll: Orbis Books, 2006).

Jose A. Pagola, *Jesus: An Historical Approximation* (Miami: Convivium Press, 2012).

Ruth Page, *God and the Web of Creation* (London: SCM, 1996).

E. P. Sanders, *Jesus and Judaism* (London: SCM, 1985).

— *The Historical Figure of Jesus* (London: Penguin Books, 1995).

Edward Schillebeeckx, O.P., *God Among Us. The Gospel Proclaimed* (New York: Crossroad, 1983).

— *God is New Each Moment* (New York: The Seabury Press, 1983).

— *Jesus in Our Western Culture* (London: SCM, 1987).

— *Church. The Human Story of God* (London: SCM, 1990).

Sandra M. Schneiders, *The Revelatory Text. Interpreting the New Testament as Sacred Scripture* (San Francisco: Harper, 1991).

— *Written That You May Believe: Encountering Jesus in the Fourth Gospel* (New York: Crossroad, 1999).

Claus Westermann, *Prayer and Lament in the Psalms* (Edinburgh: T. & T. Clark. 1981).

— *Lamentations: Issues and Interpretation* (Edinburgh: T. & T. Clark, 1994).

Also by Wilfrid Harrington

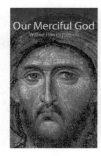  

www.DominicanPublications.com